99.9 Ways to Travel
Switzerland
Like a Local

Baden's city tower decorated for Swiss National Day.

99.9 Ways to Travel
Switzerland
Like a Local

By Chantal Panozzo

*Photographs by Brian Opyd, Wojciech Jarosz,
and Chantal Panozzo*

Cross Border Content Inc.
Chicago – Zurich – Somewhere In Between

99.9 Ways to Travel Switzerland Like a Local
by Chantal Panozzo

First published in 2017
Copyright © Cross Border Content Inc. 2017

Photos by Brian Opyd, Wojciech Jarosz, and Chantal Panozzo
Edited by Jennifer Rose Smith and Perry Iles
Cover design by Michael K. Wright
Book design by JD Smith
Map design by Jamin Hoyle

Print: B&W Edition

ISBN 978-0-9903155-3-7 (Print),
978-0-9903155-6-8 (Print: B&W Edition),
978-0-9903155-4-4 (Kindle),
978-0-9903155-5-1 (E-book)

To my American husband and Swiss-born daughter, with whom I have shared most of the adventures in this book. May travel be a gift we keep unwrapping.

Introduction

Not long ago, I read an article by American travel writer Rick Steves in which he said: "Orlando is for people who cannot handle reality. Go there once, but come on. It's just as important in your travels to get a dose of reality."

This got me thinking, because there are some parts of the world where reality is as beautiful as it is important. Switzerland is like that. And since I had the opportunity to live in Switzerland for almost a decade, Swiss reality and I got to know each other pretty well. Luckily, Swiss reality comes with castles.

But I admit it—even I once took a bus tour of Switzerland, a tour that took me to Lucerne and Zermatt, as if these two places alone would be enough to check Switzerland off my travel itinerary. But once I came to live in the country I learned something: there was a lot more of Switzerland to see—and my tour bus itinerary had little in common with the places the Swiss themselves went. My Swiss neighbor went to Arosa. My Swiss copywriter colleague cross-county skied in Oberwald. And my best Swiss friend, Tom, vacationed in a place in canton Ticino that didn't even have electricity. At 45, he had still never visited Zermatt.

The Swiss are as diverse as their landscape. This is not just a country to ski in and out of. It's a place where you can learn to play the alphorn. It's a place where there's a hiking sign ready to help you explore a new part of the country no matter where you are. And it's a place where you can plan a barbecue location in advance in order to have a proper Swiss lunch mid-hike.

So go ahead, dare to travel local. Predict the summer weather from a snowman. Shop at a Swiss farm store. Eat British cheese in the land of Gruyère. The Swiss do all of these things, and if you experience a little Swiss reality you'll experience something bigger about the world. Traveling like a local opened my imagination and changed my worldview. And that's why I wrote this book—so travel can do the same for you—whoever you may be. Whether you're a tourist rethinking your version of touring, an expatriate who wants to get to know your adopted country on a deeper level, or even if you're Swiss yourself. This book is for anyone who believes that the best travel stories come from a desire not just to take a snapshot of a place from a train window, but to stop, smile, and disembark for a while in order to bring the meaning of that blurry photo into sharper focus.

99.9 Ways to Travel Switzerland Like a Local is one part travel book, one part culture guide, and total bucket list enjoyment. It'll teach you where to let loose (for organized reasons) in a country wrongly accused of being uptight, what's exciting in a country stigmatized as being boring (think dressed-up cows), and how to make the most of your time and money in a country rightly known for watches and banks.

Welcome to Switzerland, un-tourists of the world. You're going to like it here.

The Internet is Your Local Travel Friend

This author trusts you, *mitenand*, to cross-reference your plans with that little thing called the Internet before you embark on any of the journeys suggested in this book. While every attempt has been made to provide the most current information, sometimes things change—even in Switzerland. So please travel like a local: check things like opening times, weather, walking routes, and train timetables (all of the activities in this book are accessible via public transport) before you go. Truly, it's part of the fun. Besides, planning ahead is a Swiss thing to do. That's why this book includes links to local websites. While most of these are in the area's local language, there are often drop-down options for many other languages, including English.

In the back of this book you'll find additional tips on using the public transportation system, ideas for saving money, various indexes to help you choose your activities, and more.

The car-free village of Gandria.

Contents

1. Take Back Row Seats at the Fire Parade — 1
2. Go to Alphorn Camp — 4
3. Ski on "Flat Land" — 7
4. Admire Flowers (Other than Edelweiss) — 10
5. Sleep Between a Waterfall and a Lake — 13
6. Experience a Tiny Fishing Village with a Larger-Than-Life Atmosphere — 16
7. Watch a Snowman Explode — 19
8. Let Loose for an Organized Reason — 23
9. Follow the Cows Home — 26
10. Party in a Tunnel — 29
11. Bike 50 Kilometers for Fun — 31
12. Be Seen at a Picnic — 33
13. Eat Vegetarian Food Inspired by Meat — 35
14. Take a Shower in a Parking Garage — 38
15. See Why Canton Aargau is Cool — 40
16. Cheer on Your Favorite Farm Team — 43
17. Spectate at a Schwingfest — 46
18. Eat Brunch with 1,000 Strangers — 49
19. Mingle Barefoot — 52
20. Discover How Swiss Celebrities are Made — 54
21. Find Out Why Swiss Brands are More Famous than Swiss Celebrities — 56
22. Spoil Yourself with Unspoiled Nature — 58
23. Order Potatoes with a Side of Politics — 61

24.	Drink in a Secret Garden	63
25.	Consider Monday Night Skate an Olympic Event	66
26.	Study the Grandeur of the Abbey Library	69
27.	Swim Across a Lake	71
28.	Talk to a Sculpture	73
29.	Join the Circus	75
30.	Walk on a Wine Trail	78
31.	See Why Flying is Beautiful	81
32.	Enjoy Surprisingly Un-Swiss Prices	84
33.	Playground and Language Hop	87
34.	Snowshoe to Fondue	90
35.	Admire a Castle Fit for a Mouthwash King	94
36.	Hike with No Tourists	96
37.	Experience Red Carpet Treatment	98
38.	Grill Sausages at 534 Fire Pits	101
39.	Don't Bargain at the Flea Market	104
40.	Eat British Cheese in the Land of Gruyère	107
41.	Read *A Bell for Ursli* and Hike the Story	109
42.	Bathe in a Brewery. Or a Church.	112
43.	Go to Liechtenstein (Because You Can)	115
44.	See Why the Swiss Riviera Deserves its Name	118
45.	Drink to Swiss Wine Being Rarely Exported	120
46.	Lounge by Lake Cauma and the Swiss Grand Canyon	123
47.	Discover Why Swiss Cheese has Holes	126
48.	Relax for Exactly One Minute	129

49.	Border Shop	131
50.	Hike on Slippery History	134
51.	Walk in the Snowy, Candlelit Woods	137
52.	Celebrate Static Electricity	139
53.	Watch Hot Air Balloons Sway to Yodeling	142
54.	Bike to the Top (and the End) of the World	145
55.	Ride the Highest Exterior Elevator in Europe	147
56.	Go on a Free Drinking Tour	149
57.	Take a Lesson in Humility at a Schoolhouse	151
58.	Pray to the Black Madonna	154
59.	Have Breakfast in a Bath	156
60.	Photograph 22.6 Kilometers of Ice	159
61.	Eat Chocolate and Cinnamon-Roasted Pumpkin Seeds	162
62.	Gaze at the Madonna del Sasso for a Heavenly View	164
63.	Drink Beer While Small Children Carry Flaming Turnips	166
64.	Pick Flowers, Fruits, and Berries	169
65.	Walk Through 26 Cantons	172
66.	Shop at a Farm Store	174
67.	Go Hunting and Gathering	178
68.	Walk the History of Two Countries along Castle Ramparts	180
69.	Learn Gardening Secrets with the Lazy Gardener	182
70.	Transport Yourself through Transportation History	184

71. Leave Lake Lucerne to the Tourists (and Go to Lake Lungern)	186
72. Play Politics at the Parliament	189
73. Admire Art and Architecture	192
74. Mingle with Movie Stars	195
75. Tee Off over the Highway	197
76. Eat Cotton Candy While Kids Shoot Guns	200
77. Say "Ready, Set, Moo" at the Cow Races	202
78. Swim in a Postcard	204
79. Ice Skate to Candlelight and Hearts	207
80. See How a Landslide Became a Landmark	209
81. Watch Swiss Street Artists Work	211
82. Eat 49 Kilos of Bread	214
83. Sled Down a Mountain in the Summer	216
84. Watch Caroling Being Redefined	218
85. Attend a Cow Fight	220
86. Enjoy a Rare Swiss Smile	222
87. Discover a City Within a City	225
88. Sled to the City	227
89. Admire One of the World's Most Expensive Christmas Trees	229
90. Buy Fabric Fit for a Queen. Or a Hollywood Movie Star.	232
91. Get Lost in Time in a Country Known for Timekeeping	235
92. Listen to Classical Music in a Classic Mountain Village	237
93. Go to a National Park in a Country that is a National Park	239

94.	Ride the Rhaetian Rails. Then Photograph Them.	242
95.	Visit the Most Beautiful Place in Switzerland	245
96.	Shop for Reincarnated Rubber	248
97.	Do Three Sports along a Lake that Borders Three Countries	250
98.	Tour Zurich's Sweet Side	254
99.	Ride the Bernina Express to its Highest Point	257

99.1-99.9 ADDITIONAL RESOURCES		261
INDEX OF IDEAS BY		
	99.1 TIME OF YEAR	261
	99.2 TYPE OF ACTIVITY	267
	99.3 LOCATION WITHIN SWITZERLAND	274
99.4	USING THE SWISS PUBLIC TRANSPORTATION SYSTEM	280
99.5	SAVING MONEY IN SWITZERLAND	282
99.6	SPEAKING SWISS	285
99.7	KEEPING THIS BOOK ACCURATE	291
99.8	USEFUL WEBSITES	292
99.9	ABOUT THE AUTHOR	294

INDEX	295
ACKNOWLEDGMENTS	303
Say Hello. Or Grüezi.	304

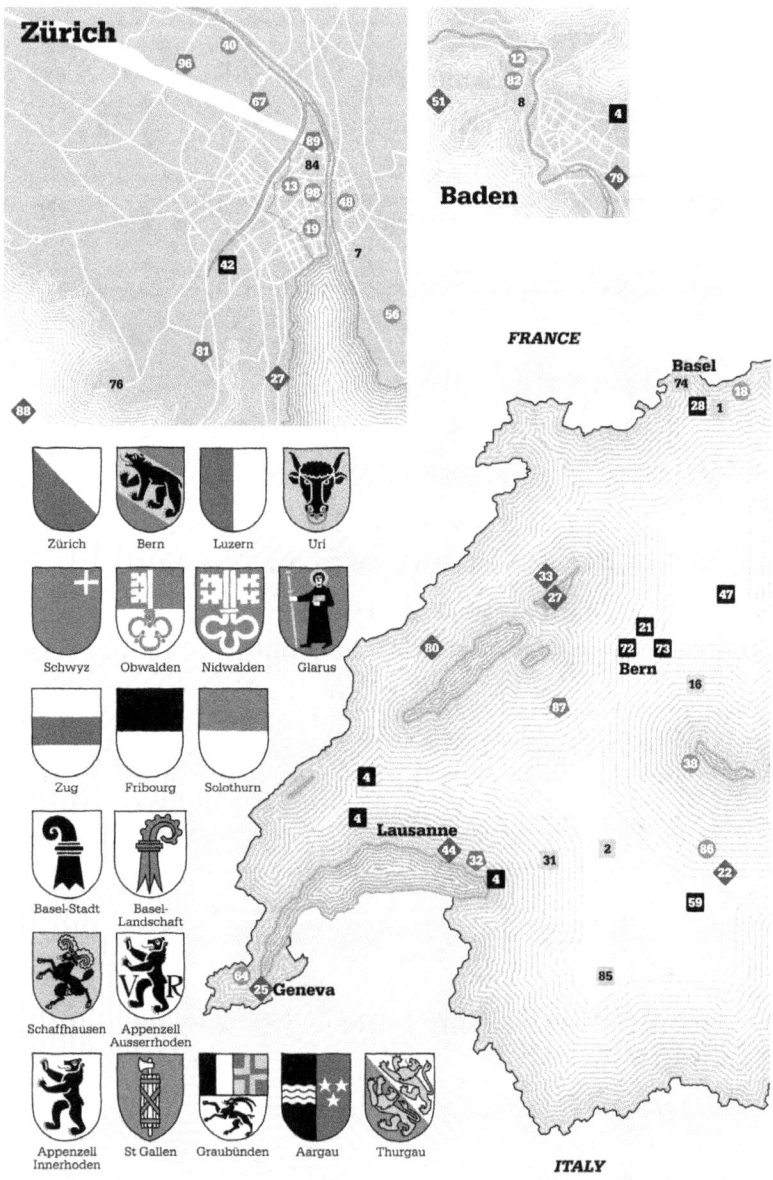

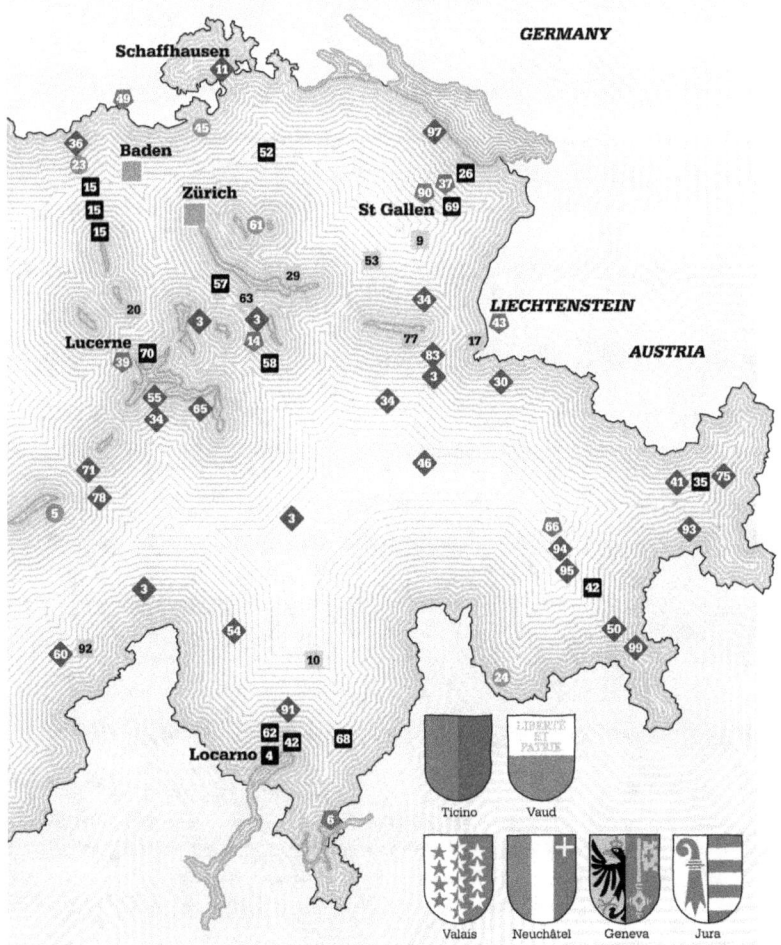

1. Take Back Row Seats at the Fire Parade

Celebrate carnival by taking back row seats at Chienbäse.

Achtung! Sparks! Get out your metal colander, un-tourists of the world, because *Chienbäse* is one parade where not following the dress code could get you burned. So go ahead, wear your colander like a hat, wrap your coat in aluminum foil, put on some oven mitts, and celebrate the prelude to carnival like you've never done before.

Kitchenware becomes kitchen-wear every winter in Liestal for good reason: *Chienbäse*, part of a long history of bonfires before Lent, is not your everyday parade. It's a 1.6-kilometer procession where participants carry flaming broomsticks, teams of men pull mobile bonfires, and spectators not wrapped in protective headwear and aluminum foil feel the sparks. Yes, *Chienbäse* is a parade that leaves you blowing ash from your nose, a parade where only the tourists without the benefit of this book take front row seats, and where the road is covered with paper confetti to make the sparks and any displaced flaming logs all the more exciting. Safety is not the point. Fire is. In fact, the warmth generated from one of the parade's fire wagons could heat a house for an entire winter.

The evening parade, which first took place in its current form in the early 1900s, is called *Chienbäse* for good reason. The word translates to "pine brooms" and about 300 people carry 50-kilogram flaming bundles of them along the parade route. It doesn't take long for 21.55 square meters of wood to ponder its new existence as ash.

Due to the parade route's narrow streets, you'll want to arrive early to get a coveted back row seat so you can enjoy the parade without the possibility of third-degree burns. But if being doused with water by a fireman sounds exciting, then go ahead, take a front row seat. Medical professionals and those who fight fire for a living will be waiting for you in large numbers—this is a parade that comes with public health warnings.

Despite the danger, you can expect crowds as big as the flames. And don't worry about Switzerland's culture of litigation—it's practically non-existent. That's why Switzerland can take words like fire, fun, and public, and combine them into one hot event. Enjoy it responsibly, *mitenand*.

Tips:

1. Come early for back row seats.

2. Animals and children under six years are discouraged along the parade route (but children carrying flaming broomsticks in the parade are encouraged).

3. If you're hungry, do what the locals do: bring your own sausage and grill it over the passing flames.

4. Fireworks are prohibited (but cigarettes and cigars are welcome).

For more information:

www.chienbaese.ch

When:

Yearly, the Sunday following Ash Wednesday

Where:

Liestal (near Basel)

2. Go to Alphorn Camp

The alphorn has no finger holes, tubes, or valves.

There's no better place to learn to play the alphorn than on the Horn Mountain near Gstaad. Here, the Hornberg is your stage, the cows are your audience, and the Hotel Restaurant Hornfluh is your après-horn, serving you that well-earned drink after a hard day of practice.

Fritz Frautschi founded the Swiss Alphorn School over twenty years ago and offers courses in the Bernese Oberland. He credits the popularity of his alphorn classes with people's desire to get back to nature. Unfortunately, learning to blow one of the world's largest wind instruments isn't so natural. The alphorn is 3.5 meters long and has no finger holes, tubes, or valves, so all note variations are controlled by the speed and force of your lip vibrations on the mouthpiece. According to one student, the more you kiss your spouse, the easier blowing the alphorn becomes.

It's much easier to learn the alphorn if you've previously played an instrument like the tuba or trumpet. But regardless of your musical experience, Frautschi prioritizes teaching you how to make a lovely sound—which is great, because a beginner playing the alphorn often produces a sound that resembles a dying cow. And speaking of cows, the alphorn attracts them. Play a few notes (good or bad) and cattle come calling. The alphorn is how the farmers bring their herds home and how you, the non-farmer, can entice an unintentional but very committed audience. Tourists may flock to you as well. And if this author's experience counts for anything, you don't have to be a master player to get a following.

As well as attracting cows and tourists, the alphorn also inspires Swiss conversation. The instrument's history may have a lot to do with this; besides bringing the cows home, the alphorn was also used to communicate with fellow herdsmen across many valleys. This author once called the alphorn "Switzerland's secret social networking tool" because all the normal cultural formalities that apply in Switzerland are set aside if you carry an alphorn. Fellow alphorn players, strangers or not, are always on first-name terms with each other. So if you've always wanted to get to know a particular Swiss person better, now you know what to do.

Come home from alphorn camp and play the Swiss national instrument on a city street, and you will have discovered the key to Swiss culture (and perhaps a nice source of income).

For more information:

www.alphornatelier.ch

www.alphorn.ca/school.htm

To buy an alphorn:

Musik Kollegger in Davos

www.musik-kollegger.ch

3. Ski on "Flat Land"

Switzerland has many groomed cross-country skiing and skating trails.

There's more to winter in Switzerland than Alpine skiing. In fact, why not enjoy a Swiss winter *sans* Alpine skis? Because when it comes to skiing (among many other things) Switzerland is neutral. It is groomed for both downhill and cross-country skiers, and as far as the Swiss are concerned, some of their terrain is perfectly flat. You'll just have difficulty finding it if you are from the ultimate in flat landscapes—like this Illinois-born author.

Below are five areas for cross-country skiing that can make almost anyone fall in love with the other, less-expected version of Swiss winter wonderland.

Disentis-Trun

In this fairytale Romansh-speaking area of Switzerland, you can ski a 15-kilometer cross-country trail of medium difficulty.

It runs between the villages of Disentis and Trun, but you can choose your own finish line thanks to strategically placed train stations that run along the valley. Also: If you're not quite a local yet, don't be put off by the trail's initial steep descent—it flattens out about 2.5 kilometers after Disentis. As a bonus, this trail isn't too well traveled, allowing you to admire the picturesque landscapes in your own private snowy storybook. www.disentis-sedrun.ch

Oberwald-Niederwald

From Oberwald to Niederwald, you can ski an easy 22-kilometer groomed trail through twelve photogenic villages in the Goms Valley. If you get tired halfway, all the better, as you'll have many options for a hot chocolate break. It's also easy to take a train ride to and from almost any of the villages on the Matterhorn Gotthard Railway. There are many other trails in this area too, including one that allows dogs to ski with you as well as a route between Obergesteln and Ulrichen that's illuminated after dark. www.obergoms.ch

Einsiedeln

Einsiedeln has a lot to offer cross-country skiers of various abilities, including the advantage that there is not an Alpine skier in sight. The Schwedentritt trails begin near Einsiedeln Abbey and are easily accessible whether you take the train or drive (Parkhaus Brüel is a parking garage near the trails that comes complete with changing rooms and showers—see Idea 14). Ski rentals and a small café can be found at the trailhead. Choose your distance (from 2 kilometers up to a half marathon) and follow the trail signs. Because of their proximity to Zurich, these trails tend to be busier than many of the others listed above. www.einsiedeln-tourismus.ch

Flumserberg

Take the lift up to Tannenboden with the downhill skiers. Ignore their looks of superiority. The classic 4-kilometer loop at Alp Tannenboden is for skaters too, and is short but picturesque. It's also quite an adventure in icy conditions thanks to its ups and downs. As you ski through the clouds, dog sleds will probably race past you. Bonus: This trail is a good pick for those with downhill skiing partners because you can both do your sport of choice and meet for lunch at the mountain restaurant. The downside? The rentals can be expensive up here and you'll have to walk a bit to get to the trail from the station in Tannenboden. Those skating (as opposed to classical skiing) will have a few additional short trail options. www.flumserberg.ch

Zugerberg

Berg means mountain, and the *Zugerberg* is true to its name. Cross-country skiing on this mountain overlooking Zug and its eponymous lake involves a lot of ups and downs. And they are big altitude changes—at least as far as American Midwesterners are concerned. Either way, Zugerberg is worth a visit—even at night since it offers an illuminated 1.1-kilometer trail for both classic and skating skiers. Daytime trails include an 11-kilometer classic loop and an 11.5-kilometer skating loop. Neither is recommended for complete beginners who are not used to the Swiss definition of "flat land." www.loipe-zugerberg.ch

4. Admire Flowers (Other than Edelweiss)

Yellow rapeseed fields near Wettingen.

Eight years. That's how long this author searched for edelweiss in Switzerland. And she found quite a bit of it. She found it embroidered on shirts. She found it decorating bread bags. And she found it for sale in the plant department at the local Migros grocery store. But never once did she see edelweiss where she wanted to see it: in the wild.

Later, she discovered there was a reason for this—edelweiss has been picked so often over the last 200 years that it has reached the point of extinction. There are still some sightings in the Swiss National Park (see Idea 93), but if you never find a single flower in its natural habitat, that's completely normal. Whew.

To make up for the lack of edelweiss, there are many other flowers to be found in Switzerland. Springtime brings so many varieties, you can create your own Swiss spring flower tour.

Tour One
Camellia Gardens of Locarno

For the largest display of camellias outside their home country of Japan, be sure to visit Locarno in March and April, when almost all of its 850 varieties of camellia plants are in bloom at the Parco delle Camelie. It's easy to soak up the atmosphere (and the sunlight) since the park hugs Lake Maggiore. Locarno likes to brag that it's the sunniest place in Switzerland, averaging over 2,100 hours a year—that's nearly six hours a day. This author, however, always ends up in Locarno in the rain. If you find yourself as unlucky as yours truly, Locarno's Visconteo Castle hosts a camellia exhibition in the early spring featuring over 300 varieties expertly arranged by professionals. www.camellia.ch

Tour Two
Rapeseed Fields of Switzerland

Every April and May, blankets of gold cover the Swiss countryside. Rapeseed fields are to Switzerland what lavender is to Provence—except without the crowds or the clichés. In fact, rapeseed is the most significant home-produced oilseed—over 8,000 farmers grow it and you'll find the yellow fields spread across 15,000 hectares throughout the country. Take a drive, ride a bike, or go for a walk through some of Switzerland's flatter and more low-lying regions and you'll be sure to discover a field. Wettingen, not far from Zurich, is a lovely area to explore. Take Bus 3 from Baden or Wettingen train station to Brunnenwiese and walk about five minutes east until you come upon the fields and hiking trails. In the French-speaking Romandie area, the fields around La Sarraz are usually blanketed by rapeseed plants as well. The medieval castle in La Sarraz offers wonderful views over the surrounding countryside.

Tour Three
Narcissus Fields Near Montreux

Despite local claims that the narcissus is becoming as rare as the edelweiss, narcissi can still be found in the wild—if you know where to look. French-speaking tours of narcissus fields are available in Montreux, but it's easy enough to create your own tour. A good bet is to take a 20-minute train ride from Montreux to Caux and then hike up from there until you come upon a glorious field of white. The best time to spot narcissus blooms is usually from the end of May through the first week of June.

Tour Four
Iris Fields Near Morges

For a final flower adventure, head to Les Jardins du Château de Vullierens in May or June. The castle is truly in the middle of nowhere, but that doesn't stop the Swiss transportation system, which can deliver you straight to the iris festival. From Morges, you can take a 16-minute PostBus ride to Vullierens Village. (Tell the driver where you are going when you get on so you're sure to get off at the right place.) Once you arrive at the castle and pay your entry fee, you'll be free to wander the iris fields, enjoy pastries from the castle café, or buy some iris bulbs for your own garden. Be sure to check the bus departure times—while you can count on it to show up on time, the bus has more in common with a lazy French schedule than a demanding Swiss one—especially on the weekends. www.jardindesiris.ch

5. Sleep Between a Waterfall and a Lake

The view at the top of the waterfall is worth the climb.

Depending on the year and the survey, Zurich often takes the prize for being the most expensive city in the world. Even the most basic hotel room in Zurich can cost over 200 SF a night, and a plate of melted cheese can be over 30 SF. Leave Zurich and it doesn't get much cheaper. High Swiss prices can make a tourist wonder if Switzerland is worth it. But because this book is both a travel and culture guide, it's this author's job to make you Swiss enough not to care about price. For reasons unknown to the rest of the world, the Swiss are about as price-insensitive as a people can be. Are you ready to be Swiss?

Great. Then put away any remaining tightwad tendencies and allow me to welcome you to Grandhotel Giessbach, located on a cliff above Lake Brienz in central Switzerland.

Your arrival will be almost as dramatic as the hotel's setting.

To get to the hotel using public transport (and yes, of course it is possible to get to a hotel on a cliff in the middle of nowhere via Swiss public transport), take a boat across Lake Brienz. While you admire the turquoise waters and the surrounding Alps, the Grandhotel Giessbach will creep into view alongside the 400-meter Giessbach Falls, stealing the show from the rest of the scenery—but don't worry, the rest of the scenery is used to being upstaged. The Belle Époque hotel has been admired and visited by emperors, kings, and diplomats since it was built in 1873.

Naturally, the hotel has its own boat stop, and that is grand too. So is the oldest working funicular in Switzerland, which will take you and your luggage up the mountain to the hotel. It's hard to believe that the hotel closed its doors in 1979 and was considered for demolition—until Franz Weber, a Swiss ecologist, saved it from destruction in the early 1980s, and began to restore the Grandhotel Giessbach to its former glory.

But why live in the past when there is champagne in your future? Today you should do nothing except sit on your balcony (or on the hotel's porch) and enjoy a bottle of bubbly along with the setting. If the waterfall beckons (and it will, unless its constant cascading lulls you to sleep first), plan a hike to the top of the waterfall before you uncork the bottle.

This is Switzerland, a country whose national pastime is hiking, so of course there are marked footpaths from the hotel to the waterfall. Pack hiking books and a camera, because near the top of the waterfall you'll find an amazing view of the hotel that will make every single Facebook friend jealous. And if you want to keep exploring, there are several recommended hiking routes for all experience levels (some are even suitable for strollers) surrounding the hotel. Other things to keep you busy include a natural swimming pool, a garden, e-bikes, and the hotel's three restaurants, including Le Tapis Rouge, a gourmet dining destination.

For more information:

Grandhotel Giessbach
3855 Brienz
+41 (0)33 952 25 25
www.giessbach.ch

6. Experience a Tiny Fishing Village with a Larger-Than-Life Atmosphere

Gandria's back streets.

Gandria, Switzerland. Enjoy the temperate climate, the Mediterranean vegetation, and the relaxed (for the Swiss) lifestyle, and you too will have discovered another way to say *la dolce vita*.

Si si, the locals speak Italian in this cliff-hanging fishing village on the shores of Lake Lugano in Ticino, which makes it easier than ever to fall in love with Switzerland—even if you're doing so within an arm's reach of Italy. Whether you arrive by land or by lake (boats enter directly into the homes here), you'll be sure to enjoy the geraniums spilling from almost every window, the car-free village center, and the tiny streets with the big views.

Time slows down in Gandria. Brief appearances of slight disorder sometimes slip across the border. If the geraniums weren't so evenly trimmed, you might think you'd crossed into Italy. It's pretty laid back here—funny how that happens when a village is as beautiful as its location. So why not spend an afternoon enjoying an Italian meal served with a side of Swiss hospitality at the Ristorante Antico Gandria? The trout is fresh, the service is friendly, and there are swans swimming by your lakeside table.

You could also step inside the perfectly preserved 1645 chapel of San Rocco, or wander in and out of shops smaller than some American parking spaces, and walk back to Lugano via chestnut forests. Follow the Olive Path for an education on the history of olives, and to find out how easy it is to lose track of time—even in a country known for its watches.

For more information:

Ristorante Antico Gandria
Via Cantonale
6978 Gandria
+41 (0)91 971 48 71

Olive Path (Sentiero dell'Olivo)

This lakeside path is lined with restored olive groves and multi-lingual signs. The 45-minute trail goes from Gandria to Castagnola. (From Castagnola, it's another 30-minute walk to Lugano—or you can take a bus.) Be sure to notice the "Olivo di Carlin," the 10-meter olive tree in Gandria.

7. Watch a Snowman Explode

How fast the snowman burns predicts the summer weather.

When tourists who have not yet read this book think about Switzerland, they probably picture chocolate, cheese, and skiing the Alps. They don't imagine a snowman being burned at the stake to predict the summer weather.

But that's one more reason to come to Switzerland in the spring. Not to run through Alpine meadows full of virgin wildflowers. Not to see Heidi's house and the apple tree blossoms burgeoning around it. Not to eat cheese and chocolate. But to witness what most people never will—a 3.4-meter snowman being burned to oblivion.

The snowman who meets this unfortunate fate—the Böögg, in Swiss German—is part of Zurich's spring festival, Sechseläuten. The holiday has been celebrated in its current form since the end of the 19th century, and it's one of the many reasons to forget sweet little Heidi and enjoy Switzerland's less predictable side.

The word Sechseläuten means, "the ringing of the six o'clock bells." The holiday celebrates 6 p.m. because in medieval times, the workday ended at that time during summer hours. Due to the increased number of daylight hours beginning on the Monday following the vernal equinox, people not only had an extra hour to work, but they also had extra sunshine for leisure pursuits. In 1952, the holiday was moved to the third Monday in April instead of being celebrated on the first Monday after the vernal equinox.

To celebrate summer hours and predict the coming weather, you'll stand on Zurich's main shopping street watching a parade of costumed guild men on horseback, girls in flowered headdresses, and bands all marching with a single purpose in mind towards one destination—the Sechseläutenplatz (in front of the Zurich Opera House), where the Böögg (and the Swiss) await their fate.

The Böögg is no ordinary snowman. He's made of straw and cotton wool and filled with explosives. Over three meters high and a fireman's worst nightmare, he's set ablaze when the church bells ring the hour at 6 p.m. Guild members thunder around the pyre on their horses, bands play the official festival tune, and crowd members eat cotton candy as they all look forward to the snowman's quick and painless death.

Swiss folklore says that the longer it takes for the Böögg's head to explode, the longer it will take for summer to appear. It's sort of like a twisted version of America's Groundhog's Day. Sechseläuten is a very Swiss holiday because it's based on one of their favorite things—time.

Ideally, a quick explosion of the entire head and neck decapitates the Böögg in under six minutes. After the explosion, it's party time, at least until the summer comes (or doesn't). So when in Zurich, do as the locals do. Come to the festival with your own *Cervelat*, or sausage. Put it on a stick. And grill it right in the center of the Böögg's embers, taking part in what may be the largest barbecue in Switzerland.

In 2008, the Böögg's head took twenty minutes to melt and another six minutes and one second for his neck to burst, a terrible showing that nonetheless resulted in a lot of well-cooked sausages. Anyhow, that year the Swiss left the event certain of a cold, hard summer.

Sure enough, July 2008 was sweater season. The Swiss, mourning the weather, dressed mainly in black.

"The summer is over," I said to my Swiss neighbor on a cold, rainy August day.

"We had no summer," my neighbor replied.

That year, the Böögg was right. He usually is.

For more information:

Sechseläuten
www.sechselaeuten.ch

When:

The third Monday in April

Where:

Central Zurich. The festivities begin with a costumed parade. This starts in the afternoon on the main shopping street, the Bahnhofstrasse. The parade continues to the Böögg's burning at 6 p.m. at the Sechseläutenplatz between Bellevue and Zurich's Opera House. To ensure you can see the Böögg, get to the Sechseläutenplatz at least an hour or two early.

Tips:

Expect crowds, especially in the afternoon. (Workers in Zurich get the afternoon off for the holiday.) Bring your own sausage to grill.

Also:

There is a children's parade the day before, on Sunday.

> **Unofficial Böögg Summer Predictor Chart**
>
> 0-6 minute explosion: Hot and sunny with no air conditioning.
>
> 6-10 minute explosion: Cloudy and warm.
>
> 10-15 minute explosion: Summer? No. Go directly from spring to fall.
>
> 15+ minutes: Possible snow showers.

8. Let Loose for an Organized Reason

A million vistors come to Baden's 10-day Badenfahrt festival.

Baden, located 27 kilometers west of Zurich, is usually a quiet spa town. But every ten years, it hosts a ten-day festival that draws a million visitors. In terms of comparative population size, imagine 475 million people descending on New York City for an event. (A number greater than the entire population of the United States.)

Why is the Badenfahrt festival so popular? The name, meaning, "Baden goes," comes from the Middle Ages when Baden's spas were a popular escape for dignitaries. During the Reformation, many Protestant Zurichers found themselves fleeing to Baden for the kind of elusive fun that only Catholics could have back then. But the real party began in 1847, when Switzerland's first train route opened. The "Spanischbrötli-Bahn," which went from Zurich to Baden, made it easy for Protestant Zurichers to come to "crazy" Catholic Baden to eat sweet pastries (like *Spanischbrötli*, for which the train was named), sing, and let loose at the thermal spas.

Swiss people tend to relax most when given an organized reason to do so. The first Badenfahrt festival in 1923 proved this to be true. Today the festival features parades, fireworks, carnival rides, several entertainment stages, and that oh-so-Swiss trust that allows a million people into an unfenced festival area knowing that they'll all buy the festival pass anyway. Besides, how can you rope off an entire city?

The Badenfahrt festival features hundreds of creatively themed food structures representing everything that Swiss industriousness is capable of. Forget a simple food tent; at Badenfahrt, the Swiss prove that the Greeks aren't the only ones to build Greek temples. The Swiss build them too, along with sand beaches, the Eiffel Tower, and Japanese Gardens. Give the Swiss some scaffolding, and they'll give you the Taj Mahal— even if its only purpose is to serve sausage for ten days.

Aside from Zurich's Street Parade, Badenfahrt is the festival to witness the Swiss as you never have before—shrieking at 3 a.m., throwing beer bottles into the street, and dancing to rap music. To experience Badenfahrt is to experience the Swiss at their most fun-loving and free. Until of course, the clock strikes midnight on the tenth day of the festival and street sweepers arrive on the twelfth ring to start cleaning up the mess, making the entire experience feel like a figment of your imagination.

Tips:

Although the main Baden festival takes place every ten years, there is a smaller version of the festival that takes place at the five year midway point for those who can't wait that long (like this author's former Swiss neighbor). Typically the smaller events don't have as many food tents or as many carnival rides, but it's hard to generalize since each festival is unique.

Large festivals: 2017, 2027, 2037, etc.
Small festivals: 2022, 2032, 2042, etc.
www.baden.ch

Spanischbrötli pastries, a specialty from Baden that dates back to at least 1780, are a featured food at the festival, but you can try the sweet buttery combination of hazelnut and carrot almost anytime at the Moser's bakery in Baden.

Moser's Backparadies
Schlossbergplatz 2
5400 Baden
+41 (0)56 222 42 55
www.backparadies.ch

9. Follow the Cows Home

The cows return from their summer pastures across Switzerland every fall.

When in Switzerland, do as the Swiss do: get up early to see cows come home. Alpabfahrt (Désalpe) is a festival that celebrates the return of approximately 320,000 cows from their summer pastures. Almost every mountain town has one. Some, like Leukerbad, celebrate the descent of sheep instead.

Whatever your migrating animal of choice may be, it'll be welcomed back to its farm with fanfare every fall. Bells will clang, farmers in traditional costumes will yodel, and tourists will take pictures. While each village celebrates its Alpabfahrt festival differently, most feature traditional music, sell local cheeses, and have sausages lined up in perfect rows on the cleanest grills in the world. Some Alpabfahrts have petting zoos and pig races too.

The most famous Alpabfahrt is in Urnäsch. Go there and you'll be transported to another world. It's a world where guys wear yellow knickers and women wear *Dirndl* and neither rush home to take off their traditional garb. Alpabfahrt is a world where cows have the right of way on both roads and rails. A world where men young and old yodel not for tourists but for the pure delight of doing so. That's what's so amazing about Alpabfahrt in Urnäsch. The procession of cows with their shiny brown coats and heavy bells and their proud farmer families is so impressive it feels like a show and tourists record it accordingly. But it's not a show. It's a major Swiss tradition that's become a minor tourist attraction, most likely for its pure authenticity.

Tag along at the end of the procession after it makes its way through town. Brave the cowpats as the farmers continue to lead their herds home. Away from the crowds, the farmers often yodel together outside their farmhouses. They don't rush inside to put on something more comfortable, neither do they change their demeanor when they're away from the tourists. I don't know about you, but I find this magically refreshing and somewhat amazing. It seems like so many things listed on tourist calendars these days are shows put on for tourists that have little meaning attached to them anymore. But the Appenzell region of Switzerland has retained its authenticity—even if the rest of Switzerland makes fun of the traditional farmers from this area. But instead of poking fun at them, we should congratulate them for keeping their traditions alive in a world that's slowly becoming more homogenous.

Tips:

Alpabfahrt (Désalpe) festivals typically take place in September.

Arrive early so you don't miss the procession through the village. Cows decide the time.

For more information:

www.myswitzerland.com

www.appenzellerland.ch

10. Party in a Tunnel

The Swiss celebrate completed construction projects like the Americans celebrate capitalism. An article in the *Baseler Zeitung* once said, "*Tunneleröffnungen werden in der Regel ausgiebig gefeiert.*" Tunnel openings are celebrated as a rule. This author couldn't have said it better. In fact, when the H2-Tunnel between Liestal and Pratteln opened, half a million Swiss francs was spent on the festival alone.

So, ladies and gentlemen, if you would like to travel like a local, it's time to set aside your souvenir cowbells and enter a newly completed Swiss tunnel for a more authentic slice of Swiss culture. Like Badenfahrt, a Tunnelfest allows you to let loose for an organized reason. What better reason to celebrate Swiss-style than reorganized concrete?

Don't know if there's a tunnel festival around? Don't worry—your sense of smell and the local hype will lead you there.

Start with a slice of cheese. Raclette has such a strong smell that it doesn't really go well in a tunnel, but that's the exciting thing about a Swiss Tunnelfest. A Swiss Tunnelfest doesn't care. The only rule? A Tunnelfest must take your senses to another level. Which explains the brass bands. And the alphorns. Sometimes playing at opposite ends of the tunnel.

What? You're going to ditch this party to go cycling instead? This author has two words for you: go back. You can even keep the bike, because some Swiss tunnel festivals feature time trials and duathlons—after all, Swiss tunnels can be pretty long. What better way to celebrate their distance than with a bike or running race? Especially since you'll probably overdose on cheese in that very tunnel after it's over.

Now, since a Tunnelfest is a bit off the tourist track—in other words, the point of this book—here are some tips for finding one. (And finding one is part of the adventure.)

Look for posters or billboards advertising a Tunnelfest.

Sniff for cheese. Listen for brass bands and alphorns doing a duet. Listen for "Tunnelfest" in up to four official languages and many more unofficial ones. Walk near tunnels and look for signs of a festival. Try Googling "Tunnelfest ch" or "Tunnelfest Switzerland." Maybe it will be your lucky day.

On June 1, 2016, the Gotthard Base Tunnel opened with what may have been the biggest Tunnelfest in Swiss history—30,000 visitors came to the festival, including half a dozen heads of state and government. The Gotthard Tunnel will be the longest train tunnel in the world by 2020, allowing train travel time from Zurich to Milan to be reduced to less than three hours. This fifty-seven-kilometer marvel was definitely something worth blowing an alphorn for.

11. Bike 50 Kilometers for Fun

Ride or skate to discover new areas of Switzerland.

To experience the real Switzerland, it is necessary to be athletically humbled. This is quite easy to achieve in a country where people grow up on an incline. Simply huff and puff up a mountain in your fancy hiking gear until a person three times your age overtakes you in their dress shoes. Or plod up a hill on a bicycle until a commuting businessman wearing a three-piece suit zooms past, leaving you to ponder the sad existence of your padded bike shorts.

Sound like fun? Perfect. Guarantee your Swiss athletic humiliation by participating in a slowUp bike ride. From April through September, there is a slowUp event almost every Sunday, which means there is an opportunity to experience the joy that comes from biking 50 kilometers for fun that often too.

SlowUp events are wonderful. In a country that has 9,000 kilometers of biking trails and another 4,500 kilometers of mountain-bike routes, the Swiss still close roads to traffic one day a week so they can bike and inline skate on them as well. To those who hate cars as much as this author does, this is a country that has its priorities straight. In any case, Swiss roads can be as nice as Swiss bike paths since they allow you to ride alongside sparkling blue lakes, through the Alps, and sometimes through multiple countries.

Bring a bike (or a pair of inline skates), or rent a bike at the train station where your slowUp event begins. (This is Switzerland so all rides begin at a place accessible via public transport.) Try to dress like an athlete, as this will heighten the experience when the Swiss Family Robinson zooms past you in jeans and sandals. For Swiss families, a ride of 30–60 kilometers is a walk in the park. For people from other cultures, it's more like an athletic event.

No matter how fit you are, slowUp rides allow you to see large parts of the Swiss countryside in an easygoing way, with free granola bars and Rivella (nice if you like Rivella, a Swiss version of soda made with whey). Also included in each slowUp event are dogs in bike carriers, men in wheelchairs racing past you, and expats like this author celebrating whenever they actually overtake a Swiss five-year-old riding up a hill.

Along every slowUp route there are many places to stop. Luckily for those not in such great shape, stopping is part of the fun. Makeshift raclette tents sprout along the route, and farms often grill sausages and set up picnic tables. It's festive and it's sporty and it might just be the most fun you can have for free in Switzerland. Depending on the route, you might be able to have a snack in several countries before you finish. And as a bonus, if you stop on a bench to eat your lunch, you'll be treated to a constant flow of "*En Guetes*" (bon appétit) from other riders. It's really quite civilized.

For more information:

www.slowup.ch

12. Be Seen at a Picnic

The Museum Langmatt is one of Baden's finest turn-of-the-century mansions.

Sip wine, listen to tango music, and soak in a little old-school European flair at the Picnic Etude in Baden. Every June 21st you'll see them: Ladies with flowers in their hair. Little boys in white collared shirts. Foreigners like this author in jeans and Birkenstocks. The Picnic Etude is the place to be seen—but only, obviously, if you realized that ahead of time.

The picnic event is held at Baden's Museum Langmatt on the longest day of the year. Bring your own picnic or order a proper Museum Langmatt wicker basket, which is filled with sandwiches, homemade salads, fruit, local specialties like *Spanischbrötli*, and a bottle of local wine. Either way you'll dine in style. The Museum Langmatt is one of Baden's finest turn-of-the-century mansions, built by Karl Moser in the style of an English country house. Adding to the atmosphere are lush gardens, a trickling fountain, and grass worth taking off your heels (or German sandals) for.

Not in Baden on the summer solstice? That's okay, you can still picnic at Museum Langmatt and even order a picnic basket with advance notice. Or you can dine at the café in the former orangery. The mansion is called Museum Langmatt for a reason—you can take a tour of the interior year-round. And it's well worth it. While you may not recognize the names of the former owners (the Sidney Brown-Sulzer family, who founded what is now ABB), you will recognize a few other famous names amongst the French furnishings inside the house. Like Degas, Monet, Renoir, Pissarro, and Cézanne.

For more information:

Museum Langmatt
Römerstrasse 30
5401 Baden
+41 (0)56 200 86 70
www.langmatt.ch

Tips:

The museum also hosts an annual Easter Egg Hunt (with some of the most gorgeous Easter bunnies you've ever seen), music programs, garden tours, and art talks.

13. Eat Vegetarian Food Inspired by Meat

Europe's oldest vegetarian restaurant continues to innovate.

One spouse wants vegetarian food and the other wants meat. Europe's oldest vegetarian restaurant has a solution for that. It's called Hiltl Tartare, Züri-Geschnetzeltes, and Cordon Bleu. All are made with meat alternatives such as tofu, seitan, tempeh, and soy sausage and prepared so expertly you wonder if you're actually eating in a vegetarian restaurant.

Which is the point. Hiltl, founded by Ambrosius Hiltl in 1898 and still run by the Hiltl family, does not serve typical "grass food." The company employs an international team and its foods are inspired not only by meats, but also by the native countries of its employees. India, Persia, China—and yes, Switzerland. The restaurant features an extensive buffet where jeera dal, barley risotto, and Arab bamja all come together in one place—on your plate.

To be sure, going to Hiltl's buffet is a kind of sporting event in Switzerland, and the game strategy can be tricky. Not only is there no order or direction around the buffet since the Swiss don't believe in lines, but there are also lots of choices to contend with. Hot plate or cold plate? Salad or soup? Vegetable paella or Sam Tam Bamee? Chocolate mousse or *Linzertorte*? If it's all too much to handle (the buffet has around a hundred dishes) and you don't feel like competing at the always-crowded buffet (Hiltl is proof that not all Swiss eat lunch only and exactly at noon), there's a menu to order from as well.

If you get tired of Hiltl's constant crowds but not of the food and trendiness, Hiltl cookbooks allow you to cook the famous recipes at home—but before you do that, you can learn from the experts themselves at Hiltl's cooking studio. As well as cooking and eating a multiple-course vegetarian meal, you can meet the man who studies meat in order to develop vegetarian dishes that make the most of its flavor—and brings in more carnivores for dinner.

Hiltl is constantly reinventing what it means to be a vegetarian. In fact, Club Hiltl, which brings local and international DJs to the restaurant's bar area, has established the restaurant on the nightclub scene.

Since 2013, Hiltl also holds the title of being the first vegetarian butcher in Switzerland. Its boutique-style butchery is just around the corner from the famous Zurich restaurant. Naturally, the butchery is every bit as modern and hip as its namesake. After all, what other butchery do you know of with chandeliers, a sitting area, and free Wi-Fi? It's worth a stop, even if you're not in the market for quorn.

For more information:

Haus Hiltl (main restaurant location)
Sihlstrasse 28
8001 Zurich
+41 (0)44 227 70 00
www.hiltl.ch

Hiltl Shop/Butchery
St. Annagasse 18
8001 Zurich
+41 (0)44 227 70 27

14. Take a Shower in a Parking Garage

When you've been in Switzerland long enough, you realize something: You can take a shower in places where you wouldn't otherwise consider taking a shower.

In a parking garage, for instance.

This author would like to ask you, dear reader: Is there any other country in the world where you would see a shower in a parking garage and think, "Yes, I might actually consider using that?"

Well, that's the case in several places in Switzerland, including Einsiedeln, where the parking garage comes complete with toilets, showers, and a locker room. And none of these facilities are questionable.

This is when you realize you love Switzerland. It's a country where you can shower without regret not only in parking garages, but also in train stations and at the airport.

It's not without reason that Switzerland is known for cleanliness. A Swiss citizen would never exercise and return to their home or office without taking a shower first. So go ahead, readers. You haven't really experienced Switzerland until you discover all the extra special places where you can become as clean as the country you're living in (or visiting).

Unexpected Places to Get Clean:

Parkhaus Brüel AG
(Especially useful after cross-country skiing on the nearby trails—see Idea 3)
Birchlistrasse
8840 Einsiedeln
+41 (0)55 412 85 13
Showers are free

McClean Hygiene Center (Train Station Shower and Toilet Facilities)
You can find these in almost all major Swiss train stations including Basel, Bellinzona, Bern, Geneva, Lausanne, Locarno, Lugano, St. Gallen, Winterthur, Zug, and Zurich.
Showers cost around 12 SF

Transit Hotel at the Zurich Airport
Flughafen Zürich AG
Gates B/D, Level 1
+41 (0)43 816 21 08
Showers available for 15 SF

15. See Why Canton Aargau is Cool

Once a count's residence, Lenzburg Castle is now owned by Americans.

Rural canton Aargau gets a bad rap from Zurich residents for being old-fashioned. But today, castles are to canton Aargau what lawyers in Armani suits are to canton Zurich. They're everywhere. And let's be honest, which would you rather have more of?

In canton Aargau there's a castle almost anywhere you look. Why? Well, in the early medieval times, Aargau was a disputed area between the duchies of Alamannia and Burgundy. Then from 1254 until 1415 the Habsburgs ruled the area, and many of the castles from that time are still standing today.

While some of canton Aargau's castles are in ruins (albeit romantic ruins you can hike through), many are well-preserved museums. Visit the 13th century **Wildegg Castle**, and imagine you're a part of the noble Effinger family living in an elegantly furnished feudal estate. This won't be hard. Wildegg Castle's impeccably preserved porcelain collection, baroque buildings, and historic gardens filled with rare flowers and plants turn any feudal fantasy into a reality.

Lenzburg Castle towers over the town of Lenzburg, and has a thousand years of history. Once a count's residence, it then became the seat of Bernese bailiffs, and finally the private home of rich Americans. A castle visit still offers hilltop views of the countryside and enjoyable walking opportunities. The castle also hosts various medieval events throughout the year. These programs, filled with costumed fun and historic food, are especially entertaining for children but too crowded to enjoy for this author.

If you're looking for a castle with a moat and grassy courtyard, **Hallwyl Castle** is reason enough to venture into canton Aargau. The castle's exhibition rooms tell the story of its history. It's only a 15-minute walk from the castle to Lake Hallwil's nature reserve, where you can end a royal day with a boat ride, a swim, or a stroll past the vineyards.

Still can't get enough castle? You're in luck, because **Aarburg Castle** is a castle built around a castle. You can't go in, since it's now a rehabilitation facility, but it's worth a trip to see its perch on a rocky hillside above the Aare River. Go on a walk, then put your feet in the green Aare while you admire this castle within a castle and you'll probably come to a conclusion much like this author—that while Switzerland may not have royalty, the castles of canton Aargau can still make you feel like a king.

For more information:

Wildegg Castle
Effingerweg 5
5103 Wildegg
+41 (0)62 887 12 30
www.schlosswildegg.ch

Lenzburg Castle
5600 Lenzburg
+41 (0)62 888 48 40
www.ag.ch/lenzburg

Hallwyl Castle
5707 Seengen
+41 (0)62 767 60 10
www.schlosshallwyl.ch

Aarburg Castle
4663 Aarburg

Bonus:

Cool helicopter video of canton Aargau's castles by Hans Fischer:
www.youtube.com/watch?v=DnKRltP8TvQ

16. Cheer on Your Favorite Farm Team

Points are given for failure in this sport from the 16th century.

There may be times of sporting confusion in your life when you can't decide between golf, baseball, and fishing. For those times, there is one word for you: Hornussen.

Who knew that one Swiss sport could solve so many of your problems? And yet, there it is, Hornussen, probably going on at an Aelplerfest right now without your knowledge. So, moral of the story: do not collect 200 francs. Do not pass go. Instead, get directly to that Hornussen match and satisfy all your sporting options.

Hornussen. The name of the sport comes from its puck, which is called a Hornuss (or hornet) because of the buzzing sound it makes when catapulted through the air at 300 kilometers an hour. Hornussen is part medieval war game and part gentlemanly golf match. Oh, and its participants dress as if they're headed to a NASCAR tailgate. This is a sport you need to see.

The game has its roots in the 16th century, when it was fun to stand on mountains and hit burning logs into valleys. Today, you can witness Hornussen matches in cantons like Bern, Solothurn, and Aargau. And don't say you can't find a match: There are over 190 Hornussen clubs registered with the Federal Hornussen Association in Burgdorf.

Hornussen is one of three traditional national Swiss sports (the others are wrestling and rock throwing—see Idea 17). Your best chance to watch the sport in a more organized, semi-touristic fashion is to attend the National Hornussen Festival or the *Eidgenoessisches Schwing und Aelplerfest*. The latter features all three traditional national Swiss sports but is only held every three years—2019, 2022, 2025, etc.

If you want to play Hornussen, you'll need one-and-a-half hectares for your field, an elastic stick resembling a fishing pole for your bat, a puck-shaped projectile (the infamous Hornuss) for your ball, and a wooden paddle for your catcher's glove. Ideally, you'll also be able to shout a battle cry in Swiss German before the game. Simple enough, right?

Got your Hornuss? Great. If you're the batting team, hit the Hornuss as far as possible (ideally, 330 meters) with your fishing pole thing into the field. Your opponents will try to catch the Hornuss with their wooden paddles before it falls to the ground. Each team gets points for failure. Play for three to four hours. The team with the least amount of failed interceptions—and therefore, points—wins. *Viel Spass, mitenand.*

For more information:

Federal Hornussen Association
www.ehv.ch

Living Traditions in Switzerland
www.lebendige-traditionen.ch

In 2015, Swissmint created a silver coin dedicated to Hornussen. Now there's a proper souvenir or gift for the Hornussen lover in your life.
www.swissmint.ch

17. Spectate at a Schwingfest

Schwingen is still an amateur sport. But that's slowly changing.

If *Schwingen*, the Swiss version of wrestling, had an advertising slogan, it might be this: Schwingen: I Smell Sport.

A Schwingen match is the perfect event to attend if you are looking for the real Switzerland. It's here that a ring of sawdust becomes a national stage. It's here that ancient rules and tradition combine with modern hype. And it's here where a rural sport from the German-speaking areas of the Alpine foothills has grown into a national phenomenon.

Despite Schwingen's long history (go to the cathedral in Lausanne for a depiction of a 13th century Schwingen grip) it's still a mostly amateur sport—even if the winners of the Federal Wrestling and Alpine Games Festival (*Eidgenoessisches Schwing und Aelplerfest*) do end up on pin-up calendars.

Schwingen matches feature fixed grips and a "uniform" that typically includes an Edelweiss Hemd (a traditional Swiss farmers' shirt featuring edelweiss flowers), pants, and a pair of burlap shorts worn over the pants. These shorts are an important part of the sport because they feature a slit in the back that allows your opponent to grab your belt and throw you (in rule-appropriate ways, of course).

There are currently around a hundred throws in the game with names like Brienzer, Kurz, and Bur. During a match, if your back and both shoulder blades touch the sawdust—and your opponent is still holding your shorts at that time—your game is over. The consolation prize? The winner will wipe the sawdust from your shoulder. Unfortunately, the humiliation is harder to get rid of.

The Swiss Schwingen Association (*Eidgenössischer Schwingerverband*) was founded in 1895 and has over 5,000 active wrestling members. These men—and, since 1980, women—typically compete for the glory of winning. What most Schwingen competitions lack in prize money, however, they make up for with awards such as young bulls, cowbells, and rustic furniture.

Some of this so-called "playing for the love of it only" attitude is changing, however, thanks to increasing sponsorship and advertising during the Federal Wrestling and Alpine Games Festival, the country's biggest Schwingen competition. This event features eight rounds of wrestling over two days. It also showcases the other two traditional Swiss sports—*Hornussen* (see Idea 16) and stone throwing. The weekend also includes yodeling, flag throwing, and alphorn playing. The competition has been held regularly since 1895 and every three years since 1974, so the next Schwingen king and queen will be crowned in 2019. Over 250,000 spectators are expected to attend this competition. Will you be one of them?

For more information:

Swiss Schwingen Association
https://esv.ch (German and French only)

18. Eat Brunch with 1,000 Strangers

The tradtional August 1 brunch takes place at 350 farms throughout Switzerland.

This author only has one regret regarding the traditional August 1 farm brunch: That she didn't discover it sooner. August 1 is Swiss National Day and there is no better way to celebrate it than by having brunch on a farm. Think endless Birchermüsli, Zopf, fresh breads, smoked meats, butter, cheese, eggs, honey, homemade jams, and Incarom coffee served over the sounds of a few loud moos and you'll get the idea. Over the last twenty years, the August 1 brunch has become such a big deal that there's now an entire website devoted to it, and Migros, one of the largest grocery store chains in Switzerland, publishes "Brunch Magazine."

Support for local farms in Switzerland is nothing new. The Swiss have long preferred to buy local products over imported ones and will gladly pay extra for the pleasure of helping their countrymen. The popularity of the brunches is just an extension of the passion the Swiss have for eating locally.

There's more to a farm brunch than food, however. Many farms offer opportunities for children to feed goats or rabbits, some have organized art projects during the brunch—make a purse out of a paper plate, anyone? Others offer entertainment such as line dancing, mini alphorn concerts, or farm tours. The goal is to bring people from the city and countryside together, which is a mission that countries like the United States would be smart to consider too.

Though August 1 has only been celebrated as Swiss National Day since 1891, the country was founded 600 years earlier on August 1, 1291 when the three cantons of central Switzerland—Uri, Schwyz, and Unterwalden—took an oath in the Rütli meadow on the banks of Lake Lucerne to establish the country. But the people of Switzerland have only been able to celebrate their national holiday work-free since 1993.

The Swiss make up for all that lost partying time with a huge spread of food followed by an evening of fireworks. To show your Swiss spirit and epitomise Swiss brunch fashion, be sure to wear the semi-required edelweiss shirt. And for your personal collection, you can also stock up on Swiss flags, Swiss candles, Swiss lanterns, and anything else you can think of that's Swiss—hardboiled eggs decorated like a Swiss flag, anyone?

To find a brunch near you, (and there most likely will be one, since up to 350 farms across the country now participate) you can search for a brunch by canton or by zip code on brunch.ch. Once you decide on a brunch location, be sure to reserve your spot ahead of time. Over 150,000 people make reservations for brunches across Switzerland, so you do not just brunch on August 1 when and if the spirit moves you. This is Switzerland, so farm brunches are highly organized—just like the country in which they take place.

For more information:

What: Brunch on a Farm
When: August 1, Swiss National Day
Time: Approximately 9:00 a.m.-1:00 p.m.
Price: Approximately 25 SF to 40 SF
Where to book: www.brunch.ch (German, French, and Italian only)
And yes: There is a brunch hotline…check the website for all your brunch news and needs.

19. Mingle Barefoot

Oxford shoes by day. Barefoot by night.

Contrary to popular belief, the Swiss do know how to kick off their shoes and relax—you just have to discover where it's socially acceptable to do so. So yes, Zurich's *Bahnhofstrasse* is filled with bankers and lawyers wearing three-piece suits that cost more than most American monthly mortgage payments. And yes, Swiss grocery stores are filled with elegant mothers wearing pearls while shopping with their toddlers.

But. Go to a lido at lunchtime and you'll find these same put-together people—you know, the ones who know how to land every stiletto-heeled step in the center of each cobblestone as they walk—stripping off their veneer to swim with the swans.

This activity, at least in Zurich, takes place at the art nouveau *Frauenbadi* (Women's bathing house). During the daytime, this wooden-decked bathing house, whose 1888 construction was based on plans from buildings in Venice and Budapest, is for women only. On sunny afternoons, buttoned up *Züricherins* bathe topless, swim in the Limmat River, or enjoy services like massages, haircuts, and henna tattoos from the comfort of their gender-specific riverside bathhouse.

But. About three times a week during summer evenings, the Frauenbadi sheds its gender preference and transforms into the place to be for Zurich nightlife. It even changes its name to *Barfussbar* (Barefoot Bar), and both men and women are invited to take off their shoes (required) and have a *Spritzer* (a glass of white wine with sparkling mineral water—recommended) and a conversation. Some nights at the Barfussbar feature live music, some feature readings, and others feature you dancing barefoot under the stars. Swimming is not allowed at night, but watching reflections of lights from the bar dance on the river is.

Oh, and if it's too cold, (below 18 °C) you can keep your Oxfords on.

For more information:

Barfussbar/Frauenbadi
Stadthausquai
Zurich
Mid-May until Mid-September
www.barfussbar.ch

P.S. In case you're wondering, Zurich's men have their own bathhouse too. It's called the *Schanzengraben*. And true to what you'd expect from a men's organization, it opens its doors to women every night during the summer in the form of the Rimini Bar.

Rimini Bar/ Flussbad Schanzengraben
Badweg 10
8001 Zurich
www.rimini.ch

20. Discover How Swiss Celebrities are Made

If you spend a lot of time in Switzerland, there is one thing you'll notice: Roger Federer. He is everywhere—not just on the tennis court. He is in gossip magazines. On billboards. And in television commercials.

Roger promotes everything. He sells coffee. He sells cars. He sells banking services. He sells watches. In fact, he sells enough things to take up this entire page if this author was forced to list them all.

Roger is busy. There isn't anyone else in Switzerland who shares his celebrity status. And that has made Roger rich. But think for a moment: Can you name another Swiss celebrity? Heidi? William Tell? Sure. But they're fictional.

Switzerland has many famous products: cheese, chocolate, watches. But its citizens seem immune to fame. Unlike many other European countries, Switzerland has no royalty to dress up and spend their tax money on (that would be very un-Swiss anyway). And unlike the United States, politicians do not become celebrities in Switzerland either (thank goodness). If you go to Bern, the nation's capital, you'll see the Swiss collective heads of state—the seven members of the Federal Council—riding the trams and buses like everyone else.

To make up for its lack of traditional celebrities, Switzerland creates them with beauty pageants. At first, Swiss beauty pageants were only for women. Organized in 1951, the Miss Switzerland pageant has produced one female celebrity every year since. Despite being a member of the Miss Universe organization, however, a Miss Switzerland contestant has never won a Miss Universe title.

In 1994, Mister Switzerland invited men who would rather wear a tuxedo than burlap shorts (See Idea 17) to become celebrities in Switzerland too. But since 2013, even this attempt at male celebrity creation has been put on hold—there's not enough money in it. Apparently, no one cares about pretty Swiss men. Roger and the *Schwingerkönig* are more than enough male celebrity for the country, at least for the moment.

The beauty contests (there is no talent section at the time of writing) for women, however, still remain popular in Switzerland, and include commentary in the Swiss tabloids weeks before the actual judging. If Mister Switzerland/Schweiz/Suisse/Svizzera ever makes a comeback, the papers will surely discuss everything they used to, from how much chest hair is reasonable (some) to whether a sense of humor is important in the winner (yes).

It's pretty amazing how hyped the beauty contests are. But then again, you can only read so much about Paris Hilton (or good old Roger) before you've had enough, and these pageants appear to be developed to channel some of the attention away from Hollywood and onto a few good farm ladies from Aargau. The pageants are also interesting for another reason: they allow you to understand Swiss democracy a little better. Here's why: The judging panel's vote typically counts for 50 percent. The audience and television viewers' votes count for the other 50 percent.

And if you can help decide who the winner is, that's all the more reason to watch a celebrity being born at the Miss Switzerland pageant. Buy your ticket at ticketcorner.ch or watch it on television. But if you go for real, don't forget to bring your cowbell to cheer on your favorite lady.

For more information:

www.miss.ch

21. Find Out Why Swiss Brands are More Famous than Swiss Celebrities

Miss Switzerland and Roger Federer aside, Swiss brands are typically more famous than Swiss people. This author has spent over a decade writing advertisements for Swiss brands, so she'd love to take part of the credit for their fame.

But she can't. Swiss brands would be famous with or without her writing, which is usually edited by Swiss people who don't like sarcasm. But this author/copywriter digresses. Think for a moment. Can you list ten Swiss brands right now?

> Here is this author's list:
> Swiss International Air Lines (Sadly, now owned by Lufthansa)
> SIGG
> Bernina
> Toblerone (Sadly, now part of Kraft)
> Lindt
> Nestlé
> Swatch
> Rolex
> Mammut
> Victorinox
> Ricola

If you're really Swiss, and therefore obsessed with detail, you'll have already noticed that this author went crazy and listed eleven famous Swiss brands. And she could keep going. Naming Swiss brands is that easy—even if you haven't spent a lot of your career writing for them.

What do most Swiss brands have in common? If you said Swissness and quality, then every Swiss brand's marketing department is now applauding. Most marketing projects for

Swiss brands are basically the same: "Get us known for quality and Swissness," they say. And it's hard to argue with these briefings, because they work.

At the Swiss Brand Museum in Bern, you can celebrate your favorite Swiss brands—and perhaps even discover some you didn't know about. The Swiss Brand Museum is in an old customs house, a UNESCO-protected property and brand-worthy in itself. It's small in size but big in concept. Even before it opened, the Swiss Brand Museum was branding. It asked different members of the Swiss parliament to choose their favorite Swiss products and then the museum put them in a *Selecta* vending machine right outside their yet-to-be-opened door.

Now that the museum is open, various Swiss brands take center stage here throughout the year, rotating in featured exhibitions since there is not enough room to house every Swiss branding achievement in this small building, let alone in all of Switzerland. Swiss brands are bigger than the country. That's quite an achievement.

The museum's permanent exhibition features twenty-two Swiss inventions. And it's something to see: Only at the Swiss Brand Museum would boxed fondue be in its own glass display box.

Naturally there's a gift shop. After all, the Swiss Brand Museum wouldn't be complete without a store that lets you take all that Swissness and quality home with you.

For more information:

Swiss Brand Museum
Grosser Muristalden 2
3006 Bern
www.swissbrandmuseum.com

22. Spoil Yourself with Unspoiled Nature

The Gastern Valley was heavily fortified and prepared as a retreat during World War II.

When Peter Rauber, co-owner of The Hayloft—otherwise known as Switzerland's friendliest place to stay (see Idea 86)—recommended I spend one of my days in Kandersteg hiking up into the *Gasterntal* (Gastern Valley), I listened. Rauber's advice might have been biased since he grew up in the valley, but he was right: it's an amazing valley to see. There are a lot of amazing valleys to see in Switzerland, but this one impresses, even if you've been to a few—or a few hundred—others.

The trip up to the Gastern Valley from Kandersteg can be taken by private car, via a mini-bus that leaves from the train station (book ahead of time), or on foot. There is an unpaved one-lane toll road complete with a very Swiss timed system through the narrow gorge. If you hike, don't walk too close to the edge of the winding one-lane road—it's a long fall off the cliff. Walking this mountain road is an adventure in itself—especially if, like this author, you decide to push your 10-month-old up the 335-meter climb in a stroller. If you do this, you should bring both a sturdy stroller and a bit of faith. You'll need it as you walk across the narrow bridge with the Kander River raging below you. The uneven tunnel that takes you through the gorge drips with dew and is shared by cars and the minibus. But once you enter the valley there's a flat, wide path waiting for you, along with something else: Magic.

One of the first things you'll notice about the Gastern Valley is the silence. Well, okay the silence and the ringing of cowbells. Even in mid-August, there aren't many signs of humanity up here. The cows, the mountains, the waterfalls, the streams—they are yours for the day. If you're an American, you'll probably be inspired to sing *The Sound of Music* as you hop across the streams. It's okay. Because no one else will witness the way you choose to spoil the unspoiled nature of the Gastern Valley.

The valley is U-shaped. It was carved out by the Kanderfirn glacier during the last ice age. The glacier now feeds the Kander River that flows through the valley before emptying into Lake Thun. From there its waters become part of the River Aare, which carries them downstream towards Bern and eventually to the Rhine.

At the end of the valley closest to Kandersteg is Hotel Waldhaus (so yes, there is some civilization up here, but only in the summer since everyone moves to Kandersteg—even the cows—for the winter). The hotel is one of Switzerland's few that still has no electricity. Lighting? Candles. Cooking? Wood-burning stove. Ambiance? Yes.

About five minutes from the hotel via a wide trail (Path 14, towards the tiny village of Selden) is an example of a high Alpine wetland where you can see Alpine newts as well as frogs and toads. Following the signs to Selden will lead you to the inevitable—a field of cows. Beyond that is a forest. Once you cross the river, turn right and walk alongside it. Soon you'll cross the river again on another bridge.

If you look closely you'll see a few suspicious-looking spoils in the otherwise innocent-looking mountainside. Bunkers have been built into some of the rocks—can you spot them? Obviously a deserted valley is also a great wartime hiding place, and this particular one was heavily fortified and prepared as a retreat during World War II.

You may also find remnants from fall 2011, when days of heavy rain caused the valley's streams to rise to record levels, resulting in landslides that cut off the Gastern Valley from Kandersteg. The valley's people and livestock had to be rescued by the Swiss Army, who sadly, were not waiting in the bunkers mentioned previously. Not everything is as perfect as it seems in Switzerland. But bunkers and landslides aside, this valley comes close.

For more information:

www.gasterntal.ch

www.kandersteg.ch

23. Order Potatoes with a Side of Politics

Did you know that a plate of Swiss hash browns can cost over 25 SF? If not, then you are not local enough yet, and you need to keep reading. Hash browns, or fried potatoes, are a Swiss specialty so they come at a special price and with a proper name: Rösti. It's hard to live in Switzerland without doing a little Rösti research, since potatoes are almost as prominent as cheese.

Go to a Swiss grocery store and you'll see what I mean—at Migros, there are no less than eighteen labeled varieties of potatoes. Raclette potatoes. Extra raclette potatoes. Baked potatoes. Budget potatoes. New potatoes. And don't forget to repeat these varieties for organic potatoes too. This is a country that swoons for starch.

Once a proper Bernese breakfast food, Rösti is eaten everywhere and at any time of day in Switzerland. For a proper Rösti, one must cook the potatoes at least a day before using them. The basic recipe uses butter, salt, and milk. Depending on the region, Rösti is also made with onions, bacon, or cheese. In Zurich, Rösti is often served with Zurich Geschnetzeltes (a local dish made with calf liver).

Some Swiss consider Rösti a national specialty. These Swiss usually live in the German-speaking areas, since most of those in the Romandie consider themselves too sophisticated for fried potatoes.

Which brings us to the Röstigraben, or "Rösti ditch." This is the invisible line between Rösti and fondue—in other words, it's the dividing line between the German and French-speaking sections of the country. True to its name, the two sides of the Röstigraben are often split on other matters than potatoes too, such as politics. The concept of the ditch emerged during World War I, when Switzerland's German speakers mainly backed Germany and Switzerland's French speakers mostly sided with the French. Look for a map of Switzerland tallying votes after proposed immigration legislation today and you'll see the clear lines of the Röstigraben. In general, the German-speaking areas typically vote more conservatively.

Now that you've digested a little potato-related politics, you'll be properly prepared to experience them at their finest—at the Röschti Farm in Schinznach-Dorf. This farm restaurant in the middle of nowhere gives you an excuse to go to canton Aargau because it alone serves over thirty varieties of hash browns, which is an impressive number of options for a country where you never used to be able to get both a Pepsi and a Coke at a single grocery store.

Look at the Röschti Farm's menu and you are looking at an example of Swiss culture and creativity. There's a Rösti of the month. And, not to be outdone, a Rösti of the season. In the spring, there's Rösti with asparagus. In the summer, there's Rösti with salad. In the fall, there's Rösti with venison. And in winter, there's both Rösti and fondue. That's Swiss neutrality at its finest, *mitenand*.

Hash browns are always happening at the Röschti Farm—the restaurant has no *Ruhetag*—it is open daily. In fact, in 2015, the Röschti Farm celebrated twenty-five years of potato pleasure. Why not join them to celebrate even more years of potato-ey goodness? *En Guete*.

For more information:

Röschti-Farm
Bözenegg 1
5107 Schinznach-Dorf
www.roestifarm.ch
Open daily

24. Drink in a Secret Garden

One of Switzerland's most beautiful villages is in the Bregaglia Valley

Two giant sequoia trees. A baroque rose garden. And a whiff of Italian flair. That's what you'll discover when you enter Soglio's Palazzo Salis garden, which dates from the 17th century. Have a coffee, have a milkshake, or order something from the grill. No matter what you like it will be served with as much style as the perfectly trimmed beech hedges that surround you.

Soglio's Palazzo Salis was built in 1630 by the Knight Baptista de Salis and became a hotel in 1876. Guests can further enjoy its secret garden by dreaming away the afternoon on strategically placed lounge chairs in the garden's private nooks and crannies.

Soglio may be a tiny town of 300 in a valley accessible only via a never-ending switchback road (sit in the front of the PostBus if that's your transport there), but its setting leaves a huge impression. The painter Giovanni Segantini described Soglio as "the threshold to paradise." And he wasn't kidding. The village is perhaps Switzerland's most dramatically situated—not that its townspeople would brag about this, since that would be very un-Swiss of them. I had to hear this claim to fame from a Texan I met in Füssen, Germany.

Anyhow, thanks to this Texan, I went to Soglio, where at an altitude of 1,090 meters there are a lot of decisions to make. Look down at the lush Bregaglia Valley? Watch the sun throw shadows on the towering peaks of the Sciora mountain group? Admire the landmark 1354 Evangelical Church of St. Lorenzo? Those who claim there is nothing to do in Soglio haven't partaken in these activities to their fullest, which, thanks to their level of grandeur, could take up an entire day.

Those who need to "do something" (I'm talking to you, fellow Americans) while enjoying the dramatic scenery could hike the five-hour Via Panoramica (Trail 796), which winds along the north side of the valley via meadows, pine forests, and reservoirs to Casaccia. Or if you want the "I hiked to Italy" bragging rights, you can take the Via Bregaglia trail from Soglio towards the Swiss village of Castasegna, which is right on the Italian border. What this hike lacks in distance, it makes up for in elevation: From Soglio to Castasegna, there is an approximately 396-meter descent through chestnut forests.

Wandering the cobblestone streets of Soglio is an activity too—the graveyard of St. Lorenzo is its own secret garden, offering one of the most camera-friendly views of the surrounding landscapes from the village. Soglio's narrow streets also offer surprises of their own, such as strategically placed pots of flowers, garden gnomes peeking at you well before you've noticed them, and public fountains where the villagers used to (and perhaps still) wash their clothes.

Need a souvenir other than pictures? Soglio is not a shopping destination, but its tiny grocery store, Alimentari Scartazzini, has wonderful Amaretto cookies, regional food products, and postcards. And a small yellow chalet in the center of town features both geranium window boxes and authentic products from Soglio like mountain herb soaps, aftershaves made from chestnut extract, and even perfume. But if you come away empty handed don't worry, Soglio isn't exactly a town you'll forget.

For more information:

www.soglio.ch

Via Panoramica (Trail 796)
www.wanderland.ch/en/routes/route-0796.html

Hotel Palazzo Salis
7610 Soglio
www.palazzosalis.ch

25. Consider Monday Night Skate an Olympic Event

Organized skates take place on Monday nights throughout Switzerland.

Every summer in Switzerland, something wonderful happens: Monday Night Skate. Roughly every two weeks from May through September, more than twelve Swiss cities and villages from across the country shut down between fifteen and twenty-two kilometers of roads for two hours of pure inline skating pleasure. At least, it sounds like pleasure. And it is, if you define fun as sweating up a hill, dead last, with the police escorts directly behind you on their motorcycles.

Like most things Swiss, Monday Night Skate is not merely amateur fun that you casually partake in—it's an organized athletic event. The Monday Night Skate organization claims that speed is not important, but the skates held in Baden that this author experienced always appeared to be an Olympic time trial. Participants sported serious expressions and all the latest skating gear. (Note: helmet, knee, wrist, and elbow pads are recommended.)

In Zurich, where the Monday Night Skate concept began, the events (which are always free of charge) can sometimes host up to 8,000 skaters—which means there are 16,000 inline skates fighting for asphalt as they race down a hill, so trust this author when she says you need to be pretty confident on skates to participate.

Anyway, once you get over how slow you are and get used to being at the back of the pack, Monday Night Skate is a great way to get a workout and experience Swiss culture. The skates officially began in 1999, when Monday Night Skate founder Jürg Hauser created a predefined route through Zurich. In 2000, Zurich became the first official Swiss city to recognize the event and offer police escorts for the tours.

One of this author's best Monday Night Skate memories was when the police in charge of the escort pulled over a man on a bicycle and gave him a ticket for riding in a pedestrian zone. Never mind the hundreds of inline skaters who were skating in that same pedestrian zone—they were participating in safe and legal fun. But the cyclist? Well, he was basically your average Swiss criminal.

Monday Night Skate usually takes place in the following cities:

Aarau
Baden
Basel
Bern
Biel
Chur
Geneva
Lucerne
St. Gallen
Winterthur
Zug
Zurich

For more information:

www.nightskate.ch

26. Study the Grandeur of the Abbey Library

Looking for a cure for a rainy Swiss day? Switzerland's oldest library, St. Gallen's Abbey Library, offers a "pharmacy of the soul." In fact, that's what's written—in Greek—above its entrance. The monks who founded the library in the 8th century considered books medicine for the spirit. Today, your prescription can be filled for about 12 SF, the price of the library's entry fee (or the cost of a sandwich at Zurich Airport).

To begin your soul treatment, slip into some comfy slippers and slide your way inside the wood-floored library, which was rebuilt between 1758 and 1767 in an elaborate baroque style. There are frescoes depicting the first four ecumenical councils of the early church. There is walnut and cherry woodwork. And there are illuminated manuscripts. It can be hard to focus. But since it's a library, start by admiring 30,000 of the library's 170,000-strong book collection—over 2,000 of which are original medieval handwritten manuscripts. More than 400 volumes are over 1,000 years old.

Collection highlights include the oldest book ever written in German, a Latin manuscript of the Gospel, the earliest known architectural drawing on parchment, and Irish manuscripts from the 7th and 8th centuries. Note that not all of the library's collection can be viewed, however.

If you're important enough, you can request to study old volumes in the Reading Room. The library is also entering the modern age by digitizing many of its ancient manuscripts, allowing them to be accessed online. Books printed after 1900 can also be checked out.

UNESCO (the United Nations Educational, Scientific, and Cultural Organization) thinks you should visit the library too. In fact, the Abbey Library became a UNESCO World Heritage site in 1983. According to UNESCO, "The high baroque library represents one of the most beautiful examples of its era." With so many words floating around in one space, it may come as a surprise that there are no words to describe the splendor of the room.

Beyond the beauty and the books, the library also features an Egyptian mummy, a replica of a giant globe representing the world in the 1500s (the original was stolen by the city of Zurich around 300 years ago and never returned), and of course, the infinite spirit of the monks.

For more information:

Stiftsbibliothek St. Gallen
Klosterhof 6D
9004 St. Gallen
www.stibi.ch

27. Swim Across a Lake

Switzerland may be landlocked, but there are so many lakes that it seldom feels that way. In canton Graubünden alone there are 615 swimmable lakes.

Swiss lakes are some of the most pleasant bodies of water in the world. They have swans. They are clean enough to swim in. And many are big enough to make swimming across a challenge. But unlike say, Lake Michigan, they are not big enough to make swimming across impossible to those who love a challenge.

Enter the very organized Swiss lake swims. Some, like Zurich's *Seeüberquerung,* come with several scheduled back-up dates due to unpredictable summer weather. Occasionally, the weather is so bad that even the back-up dates get cancelled and no event takes place at all. But when a lake swim does happen, it is a sight to see—and even participate in.

There are many lake swims in Switzerland and this author apologizes to the ones that will go unnamed here, but writing about all of them would be another book in itself. So instead, she will focus on two lakes that are sized for swimming and have their own events in July and August, when water temperatures are bearable: Lake Zurich and Lake Biel. Naturally, you can swim in both without an organized reason, but if you're the kind of person who likes organized reasons, the following swims give you two.

Zurich's Seeüberquerung takes place every July on a Wednesday, with backup dates in July and August. The swim usually starts from Mythenquai and ends at the beach in Tiefenbrunnen, a distance of 1,500 meters. Up to 10,000 people typically take part because yes, Zurich has that many physically fit people and also that many people who can take a Wednesday afternoon off work.

If you are one of them, you can simply show up before the

swim (amazingly, it is not necessary to register ahead of time for this event) and get a start time. The cost of participation is about 20 SF. The fee includes an organized transport of your clothing to the other side of the lake along with a post-swim meal, typically something carbohydrate-rich, like risotto.

Zurich's lake swims began in 1985, when 250 fifth grade students swam across the lake as part of a school event. Adults wanted in on this feat of physicality too. So in 1986, over 800 adults crossed the lake with the schoolchildren. The rest is Zurich swimming history.

Further south, every August, the Insel-Ligerz-Schwimmen Club organizes a Lake Biel swim that allows you to swim from Ligerz to St. Peter's Island and back (2.1 kilometers) or only from St. Peter's Island to Ligerz (1.1 kilometers). Some people are crazy and swim both routes, bringing their entire lake swim to 3.2 kilometers.

Rain is no excuse not to swim across Lake Biel and the event is only cancelled if there are heavy storms or lightning. Costs vary from around 28–50 SF, depending on the length of your swim and date of registration, and you need to register the day before the event at the latest. The fee includes a bottle of regional grape juice—or if you feel like celebrating after your swim, a bottle of wine.

If swimming's not your thing but nice boat rides are, be sure to take a trip across Lake Zurich or Lake Biel instead. If you have children, see Idea 33 to combine a Lake Biel adventure with playground hopping and hiking for a proper Swiss family day out.

For more information:

www.seeueberquerung.ch

www.insel-ligerz-schwimmen.ch

28. Talk to a Sculpture

Climb up—and through—a sculpture topped with red geraniums. Press big red "on" switches and watch sculptures turn, blink, and rattle. The Museum Tinguely in Basel is one of the best (and loudest) art museums in Switzerland. So go ahead, have a conversation with a sculpture. At Museum Tinguely, you're a part of the art.

Located directly on the Rhine River, the Museum Tinguely, designed by Mario Botta, celebrates Swiss painter and sculptor Jean Tinguely, who was renowned for his mechanical sculptures. His works transform everyday piles of junk into thought-provoking statements. If you're Tinguely, you collect things like a prosthetic leg in a red sock, a pot without a bottom, an old fox fur, a silver serving tray, and a nightgown. Then you take them all and suspend them from the ceiling, making them dance chaotically on command. And *voilà,* your work of art, which Tinguely called *Ballet of the Poor*, is born.

Or maybe you take an old tractor and create a sound sculpture on top of it. Collect some bells, cymbals, pots, and barrels. Throw in a garden gnome, a trash can, and some scrap iron. Then add the noise of a tractor motor, firecrackers, and smoke bombs, and mount it all on a tractor and what do you have? *Klamauk*, Tingeuly's 1979 work of art that took its last ride during the artist's funeral procession in Fribourg in 1991.

Tinguely, born in 1925, grew up in Basel and later lived in France. His works have been displayed around the world, most notably at the Georges Pompidou in Paris, at the Tate Gallery in London, and at the Museum of Modern Art in New York City, where his self-destructing sculpture, *Homage to New York*, unfortunately only partially self-destructed.

Walk around Basel and you'll also discover the artist's 1977 Carnival Fountain (*Fasnachtsbrunnen*), located at the Theaterplatz. This spectacle rightly sits on a former stage—that of the old city theater. Tinguely used some of the pieces from the demolished theater to create the ten iron figures, which spew and shoot 55,000 liters of water day and night—unless of course, it's winter, when ice sculptures form and step up for an encore.

For more information:

Museum Tinguely
Paul Sacher-Anlage 2
4002 Basel
www.tinguely.ch

Carnival Fountain (Tinguely Fountain)
Theaterplatz/Klostergasse
Basel

29. Join the Circus

Eight generations of circus magic are included in every performance.

One ticket to the Knie Circus offers eight generations of circus magic. And attending the circus every summer is almost as Swiss as fondue or grilling sausages on a stick—even though the Knie story begins in Austria.

In 1803, Friedrich Knie fell in love with Wilma, a circus performer, while studying medicine in Innsbruck. While their relationship didn't last, his love of the circus did, and the Knie Circus was born. It originally performed in Austria, Germany, and Switzerland, but thanks to World Wars I and II (during WWII, the Knie Circus was blacklisted by Germany for not flying the Nazi flag), the Knie Circus chose Switzerland as its permanent home.

The Knie Circus has stood the test of time—and for good reason. Be like Charlie Chaplin (or this author) and sit down with a bag of popcorn or an ice cream cone and you'll be treated to a show that is both enchanting and personal as well as daring and sweet (it's hard not to fall in love with the youngest Knie, Chanel Marie, who performs on a tiny white pony).

Part of what makes the Knie Circus special is the intimate family feeling it provides—several generations of the family are involved in the show, and they perform both together and as separate nuclear families. The Knie circus tent and its sawdust ring is miniature by American standards, which contributes to the small-town feel and makes even the back row a good seat.

While the circus is local and cozy, international acts like the Chinese Diabolo Girls typically add exotic flavor. David Larible, the featured clown in 2014, provided non-stop fun and laughter—without needing any of Switzerland's four official languages to get his meaning across. His gestures, facial expressions, timing, and musicianship were superb. Audience members were invited to join his act, and even though he poked fun at them for the rest of the audience's benefit, they appeared to have fun too.

The Knie Circus is the perfect show for both young and old, and for locals and foreigners alike. It travels around the country throughout the year, performing at over forty locations across Switzerland, including, yes, the hotspot of Wettingen, where this author went to see it. She highly recommends it.

Since 1958, the Knie family has also run a children's zoo (Knies Kinderzoo) in Rapperswil, a town that hugs the shores of Lake Zurich. There, children can feed carrots to the elephants, ride a pony, or enjoy the many playgrounds. It's a great place to see animals up close and interact with them. Within walking distance of the zoo is also Jucker Farm, a laid-back locale where children and adults can pick strawberries, relax with a glass of organic apple juice, or pet the goats.

For more information:

Knie Circus
www.knie.ch

Jucker Farm
www.juckerfarm.ch

30. Walk on a Wine Trail

Divided into three sections, the entire Weinwanderweg is 40 kilometers in length.

The best way to appreciate Swiss wine (other than drinking it, of course) is to hike on a Swiss vineyard trail. Thanks to Switzerland's 60,000-kilometer network of hiking trails, there is a hike for everyone, and Graubünden's *Weinwanderweg* is one of the best for winos. This Bündner Rhine Valley path is wide and easy, as if it were made for people who taste wine as they walk (or for those pushing strollers or hiking with toddlers, which sometimes has a similar effect on walking style).

May 1, which is Labor Day in Switzerland, is one of the best times to enjoy Graubünden's *Weinwanderweg*, not only because most of the flowering trees are in bloom, but also because May 1 is Day of the Open Vineyards in the German-speaking section of Switzerland.

If you're lucky enough to be there on Labor Day, make sure to stop at several vineyards as you follow the trail. Most of the grapes in this area are *Blauburgunder*, of the Pinot Noir variety. Vineyards you visit will probably produce both a light and fruity version and a sophisticated barrel-aged variety for those with more complex tastes. You're never far from a Swiss bus stop or train station on this hike; so don't hold back on tasting—there's no reason to drive here.

Especially picturesque is the town of Jenins, where the Weinstube alter Torkel offers the ideal rest spot to enjoy a glass of regional wine along with a plate of local cheeses and dried meats. It's a restaurant, so it will be open even if it's not the Day of the Open Vineyards.

The entire Graubünden wine trail, which is divided into three sections, is forty kilometers in length. Those small on time but big on wine should enjoy the *Rundwanderweg* Malans/Jenins (a circular route of about ten kilometers).

With extra time and energy, it's worth finishing the hike in Maienfeld, more for the scenery than for the Heidi legend. But if you like both Heidi and tourist traps (hey, don't feel bad, this author sometimes does) then you'll love Maienfeld—the town where Heidi's house was said to be—and yes, Switzerland Tourism has made sure that there is a house for you to visit. The Heidi Trail will lead you there. (See, there really is a hiking trail for everyone in this country.)

Another option after the wine (or Heidi) hike: Take public transport to the neighboring town of Bad Ragaz and soak your sore muscles in the Tamina Therme mineral baths. The 7,300 square-meter spa oasis offers everything from outdoor pools to whirlpool recliner baths. Now that's something to raise a glass to.

For more information:

Graubünden Wine Trail
(At time of printing there was a downloadable wine trail map here. Included on the map is a list of all the places you can enjoy the wine too.)
www.graubuendenwein.ch

Weinstube alter Torkel
7307 Jenins
www.torkel.ch

Heidiland
www.heidiland.ch

Bad Ragaz's Tamina Therme
www.taminatherme.ch

31. See Why Flying is Beautiful

Chateau-d'Oex is Switzerland's ballooning capital.

Flying is beautiful. That's what you'll be saying after a week (or a weekend) at the International Hot-Air Balloon Festival in Château-d'Oex. Think snow-covered mountains. Think Swiss village filled with chalets. Think more than eighty hot air balloons in all colors and shapes rising above it all. This is the *Festival International de Ballons*, and this is Switzerland's ultimate magic show. Located in the Swiss Romande halfway between Gstaad and Gruyères at the end of every January, it has been *très magnifique* since its beginnings in 1979.

Château-d'Oex, an Alpine village of 5,000 residents, could be called Switzerland's ballooning capital. Thanks to its microclimate, the weather is ideal for hot air balloons. In fact, the first balloon to fly non-stop around the globe left from Château-d'Oex in 1999. It was piloted by Betrand Piccard and Brian Jones. The journey took almost 20 days.

The International Hot-Air Balloon Festival features balloons and pilots from all over the world. To get the most out of the festival without staying for its entirety, choose a weekend—the festival spans two of them—and stay a night or two at a hotel or B&B. This way, you'll be able to enjoy air shows, mass ascents, and passenger flights—with the best chance at having at least one sunny day. Be sure to dress warmly, since you'll be doing a lot of standing—unless of course, you plan to watch the event while flying down a mountain on skis.

If you want to combine your ballooning trip with skiing, you may need to head to Gstaad, Les Diablerets, or Villars for your downhill debut. At only 1,000 meters, Château-d'Oex is a mid-altitude resort and global warming isn't doing it any favors. Neither is canton Vaud, which did not include Château-d'Oex in its long-term 2020 sustainable tourism strategy for the Vaud Alps, a 100 million SF investment plan to regenerate local Alpine resorts. Each year, there are 3 percent fewer skiers in Château-d'Oex, which is great if you don't want company, but not so great if the snow is slushy and the infrastructure is dated.

There are various competitions and events throughout the International Hot-Air Balloon Festival, including one that will likely redefine your concept of a hot air balloon. It's called Special Shapes, and features hot air balloons in the form of everything from bagpipe players to roosters. Order a grilled sausage, which will likely be given to you bared-handed by a Swiss child, and enjoy the show.

Speaking of children, the festival typically offers an afternoon of tethered flights, a balloon release with prizes based on whose balloon travels the furthest (aim for over 900 kilometers to win), and other shows and activities for younger guests.

Finally, with up to 25,000 pairs of eyes glued to the skies, don't forget to look down and do a little people watching—there's never been a better opportunity.

For more information:

Festival International de Ballons
Yearly, Late January
www.festivaldeballons.ch

32. Enjoy Surprisingly Un-Swiss Prices

Good deals can be found every July and January throughout Switzerland.

Hello again and welcome to Switzerland, a nation so rich it doesn't bother minting anything smaller than a five-cent coin. For a penny-pincher, the country is a complete nightmare: you're in a place where pennies fail to exist, where a glass of water can cost 6 SF, and where travel agencies advertise shopping vacations—in New York City.

According to the Consumer Protection Foundation, the Swiss pay 15 billion SF more for household goods than their European neighbors. Is it any wonder that droves of Swiss shoppers cross the borders for better bargains, costing the Swiss economy an estimated 10 billion SF a year?

But it's hard to feel too sorry for the Swiss: they also enjoy high wages and have the sort of purchasing power most countries can only dream of. Swiss prices are partly cultural: Swiss consumers are simply willing to pay more for better quality goods—and they view low-priced items suspiciously, even if the difference in quality between the two items is negligible. In fact, an American who started a custom shirt business in Zurich once told me he was advised to raise the prices of his shirts before the Swiss would buy them. So he did. And then they bought.

For the tourist (or the local) though, there are two bright spots to every "I just got Switzerlanded" story—a term coined by an online network of expats in Switzerland fed up with high Swiss prices. These bright spots come in January and July. During these two months, the rules of Swiss economics need not apply, and you can enjoy your Swiss shopping with all that Swiss quality but none of that high-priced guilt.

Think Swiss watches for half the price, clothing up to 70 percent off (in other words, jeans for normal American prices), and running shoes for less than the cost of a mortgage payment. During January and July, Swiss department stores like Manor sell everything from coffee machines to wine glasses for less than Swiss flea market prices. Something to raise a half-priced glass to, *oder*?

For a little fun, here are some of this author's best Swiss sticker shock moments:

1. 12.90 SF ($13.99) for a small container of ice cream? Quite the champagne price for vanilla, don't you think?
2. 39.90 SF ($43.27) for 116 Pampers…oh, wait, this is the *sale price* (Originally SF 59.90–$64.96)?
3. 39.90 SF ($43.27) for laundry detergent?
4. 3 SF ($3.25) for a dinner roll that's in a basket on the table even though my entrée costs SF 29 ($31.44)?
5. 5.90 SF ($6.39) for a miniscule bag of nacho chips?
6. 1.19 SF ($1.29) a minute to call customer service for the honor of giving them my business?
7. 1,600 SF ($1,735) for a baby stroller?
8. 500 SF ($542) for a *used* baby stroller?
9. 159 SF ($172) for a nursing pillow? (Sadly, I was so desperate I bought it.)
10. 35 SF ($38) for two foot-long Subway sandwiches (no chips or drinks), but a real deal considering: 35 SF ($38) for a club sandwich (a side of veggies costs more).

33. Playground and Language Hop

The hike from Twann to Ligerz takes you through the vineyards.

The longer one lives in Switzerland, or the more often one visits, the more one realizes how disappointing the rest of the world is going to be afterwards. Contributing to this phenomenon are the shores of Lake Biel. Between the towns of Twann and La Neuveville sit what may be the world's largest concentration of pristine lakeside children's playgrounds. What's even more fascinating is that as you playground hop, you will language hop too—going from Swiss German in Twann to French in La Neuveville.

Start your multilingual day of play in Twann. Have a picnic at the lakeside playground (or on a bench just outside it) and admire how you can practically sail down the slide and onto the docking steamship, which travels to all the small towns dotting Lake Biel. In the meantime, ducks will quack, almost-silent trains will race through the vineyard above the park, and bike riders will amble by.

When your child gets tired (or you recoup some of your energy), hike up the hill and through the vineyards. Head towards the neighboring town of Ligerz (about forty-five minutes). It goes without saying that the storybook views over the vineyards, town, and lake are worth the steep climb.

Once you arrive in Ligerz, you have several options. You could take the flat, lake-hugging trail back towards Twann and enjoy another lakeside playground, or take a swim in the lake along the way. Or you could take the boat from Ligerz towards Erlach, buy an ice cream cone en route, and get off at Sankt Petersinsel (St. Peter's Island—a peninsula complete with a sandy beach, playground, and café) or at La Neuveville. Jean-Jacques Rousseau spent two months on St. Peter's Island, and recalled: "I think back to no stay with such sweet longing." Closed to traffic, the entire five-kilometer-long island is accessible by boat, on foot, or by bicycle. If you're hungry for even more beauty (or just for some dinner) the island's former monastery is now a hotel and restaurant, which serves fish fresh from the lake.

Whatever detour you choose, be sure to end the day at the gorgeous playground in La Neuveville. Here, parents can admire the rose-framed lakeside views while children enjoy two sandboxes, two slides, two swings, multiple languages, and one great day out.

Tips:

This is a very sunny area without much shade, so bring your sunscreen (and your swimsuit, if you want to swim in the lake).

Every year there is a lake swim from Twann to St. Peter's Island. (Usually in August, see Idea 27.)

The towns and scenery are worth exploring for anyone, whether you have children or not.

All lakeside villages are connected by train.

The vineyards turn gold in the autumn, usually in mid-October.

34. Snowshoe to Fondue

Snowshoe your way to one of 534 fire pits for a fondue lunch.

As you will soon learn in Idea 38, there are 534 very organized fire pits in Switzerland. Why not enjoy them in the winter too?

The Swiss are very particular about their fire pits. But this does not mean that snow-covered fire pits are shoveled out during the winter just because someone like this author fancies having fondue mid-hike. However, do not let this deter you from the experience. It's officially called a snowshoe to fondue hike. And it's exactly what it sounds like. So grab your snowshoes and strap a snow shovel, a fondue pot, some cheese, and a bottle of wine on your back and let's get going.

First, you will want to research a snowshoe trail that has a fire pit along it (not hard since this author has listed several below). Make sure to know exactly where the pit is since it might be covered in snow (not hard since fire pit coordinates are detailed on the fire pit website: www.schweizerfamilie.ch/

unterwegs/feuerstellen.html). Bring the makings for both fire and fondue in a backpack (see list below) and enjoy.

Recommended snowshoe hikes with fire pits:

Dallenwil-Wirzweli (Lake Lucerne Region)

Take Swiss public transport to Dallenwil.

Take a shuttle bus or walk fifteen minutes to the Dallenwil-Wirzweli gondola. The trail marker shows the start of the hike 50 meters from the gondola station, on the right side, in the direction of the mountain chapel.

Snowshoes can be rented in Wirzweli for about 18-21 SF.

Trail: Winterwald (Wirzweli – Hexenboden – Brügelboden – Wirzweli).
Difficulty: Easy (or medium—depending on how much cheese is in your backpack).
Length: 2 km, about 1.5 hours.
Fire pit Wirzweli, Eggwald (Coordinates: 670300/196050).
Fire pit link: www.schweizerfamilie.ch/wanderungen-ausfluege/weekendtipp/feuerstelle-dallenwil-wirzweli-eggwald/
www.wirzweli.ch

Alt St. Johann (Toggenburg Region)

Take Swiss public transport to Alt St. Johann, Post.

Snowshoes can be rented at Berggasthaus Sellamatt for about 20 SF.

Take the gondola up to Alp Sellamatt.

Trail: Sellamatt-Zinggen.
Difficulty: Medium.
Length: 3.8 km, about 2.5-3 hours.
Fire pit Zinggen (Coordinates: 740950/226900).
Fire pit link: www.schweizerfamilie.ch/wanderungen-ausfluege/weekendtipp/feuerstelle-alt-st-johann-zinggen/
www.toggenburg.org/en/mountain-lifts

Weissenberge (Glarus Region)

Take Swiss public transport to Matt Station.

Snowshoes can be rented at the lift station in Matt for about 20 SF.

Take the gondola up to Weissenberge.

Trail: There are two snowshoe trails that begin about 100 meters from Weissenberge Station. They are called Waldibach & Stäfeli.
Trail Link: www.weissenberge.ch/downloads/flyer.pdf
Difficulty: Easy (Waldibach) or Difficult (Stäfeli).
Length: Either 3.5 km, 2 hours (Waldibach) or 7 km, 4 hours (Stäfeli).
Fire pits Mühlemad (Coordinates: 732425/203500) & Meissenbödeli (Coordinates: 733125/203200).
Fire pit links: www.schweizerfamilie.ch/wanderungen-ausfluege/weekendtipp/feuerstelle-matt-muehlemad/
www.schweizerfamilie.ch/wanderungen-ausfluege/weekendtipp/feuerstelle-matt-meissenboedeli/
www.weissenberge.ch

What you'll need to pack for basic fondue:

Fondue pot

Wooden skewers (or use sticks)

White wine

Pre-packaged fondue

Bread (either cut up or bring a knife)

Matches

Charcoal

Spoon for stirring

(Optional: garlic clove, kirsch, pepper, nutmeg)

35. Admire a Castle Fit for a Mouthwash King

Once the home of a Tyrolean count, a Holy Roman Emperor, and the king of a mouthwash brand.

Tarasp Castle (Chastè da Tarasp) is Switzerland's version of Germany's Neuschwanstein (which in turn is what Disney World's version of the Cinderella castle is based on). It's a castle fit for a Tyrolean count, a Holy Roman Emperor—or for the king of a mouthwash brand, as its more recent history reveals. Maybe that's why the 11th century castle, renovated by the Odol mouthwash king Dr. Karl August Lingner in the early 20th century, has the most modern bathrooms (double sinks, anyone?) this author has seen in any almost 1,000-year-old structure.

Another feature of the castle worth singing praises about? The former armory now features a concert organ with 2,500 pipes. Sadly, Dr. Lingner never heard it. In 1916, two weeks before his nine-year castle restoration was finished, he passed away. The family of Moritz, Landgrave of Hesse, owns the castle now, and by taking a guided tour, you can imagine how it would feel to own this grand piece of real estate yourself.

For the real castle highlight, however, you'll have to leave the building. The postcard view you'll have of it from the opposite hill is worth the climb. Surrounded by a mountain meadow, your panorama will include the villages of Tarasp Spargels and Tarasp Florans, and the castle itself. Watch the sunset here and the magic increases by epic proportions, even more so when you post your picture on Facebook, ultimately crowning your friends' supreme jealousy as king.

For further awe-inspiring landscapes in the Lower Engadine Valley, a forty-minute hike from the castle lookout point takes you to Piz Nair (Black Lake), where a moorland awaits you. If it's warm, you can swim in the lake. The refreshing dip doubles as a spa treatment, as locals claim the lake mud is good for the skin.

If you've got the wallet of a royal, you can spend a night below the castle at Schlosshotel Chastè Tarasp. The hotel has been in the Pazeller family for seven generations and offers majestic service. Throughout the hotel, you'll breathe in the scent of *Arvenholz*, a distinctive regional pine that's used throughout the hotel on doors, walls, and furniture—a smell that lingers in the memory too.

For more information:

Chastè da Tarasp
7553 Tarasp
www.schloss-tarasp.ch

Schlosshotel Chastè
Sparsels
7553 Tarasp
www.schlosshoteltarasp.ch

36. Hike with No Tourists

The Fricktaler Höhenweg is canton Aargau countryside at its best—hike all 60 kilometers of this blue-signed trail, and you'll have an excursion that lasts three or four days. But the 2.5–3-hour hiking section between Bürensteig, Passhöhe and Effingen is special because it offers two places to rest along the way, each of which has beer, sausages, and an atmosphere of inexplicable Swissness.

Feel like a real Swiss (even if you are one) by buying a Cervelat from the Frischluft-Oase Cheisacher (open May-October in good weather on weekends) and grilling it yourself over the already-prepared fire. Then, an hour and fifteen minutes into your hike, you'll arrive at Cheisacher Aussichtsturm for views of the entire surrounding countryside. If you're lucky—and this author was—a yodeling club will be just around the corner in the picnic area treating you to both song and *Guetzli*.

About fifty minutes from the Cheisacherturm, you can finish your hike with another drink at the Sennhütte-Stübli (open seven days a week from 10 a.m. until 8 p.m.) before continuing the last half hour to Effingen train station.

> Begin hike: Bus stop, Bürensteig, Passhöhe
> End hike: Train station in Effingen

Tips:

> This hike is also bike and stroller friendly.

> The hike can be done year-round, but the best time is in the spring, when all of the cherry trees and meadows are in bloom.

For more information:

Cheisacherturm
www.cheisacher-turm.ch

Sennhütte-Stübli
5078 Effingen
+41 (0)62 876 13 67
www.sennhuette.ch

37. Experience Red Carpet Treatment

St. Gallen's Bleicheli quarter is covered with 4,103 square meters of red rubber granulate.

In Switzerland's Far East (in other words, in St. Gallen), the red carpet is not something rolled out for Hollywood stars. Instead, it's a permanent art exhibition—and the public plays and lives within it.

Swiss multimedia artist Pipilotti Rist (born in canton St. Gallen) and architect Carlos Martinez created the "City Lounge" by covering the Bleicheli quarter with 4,103 square meters of red rubber granulate—you know, the stuff running tracks are made of—making this "outdoor living room" an unforgettable space, not only in the city but also in your mind.

The effect is as if the Raffeisenplatz has been covered with red-colored snow. Benches, tables, roads, and even a fake Porsche parked outside of Globus are blanketed with red rubber, softening their edges but still maintaining their distinctive shapes.

Come in, have a seat on a red sofa, and soak up the atmosphere. This project isn't called the City Lounge (*Stadtlounge)* for nothing. Whether you find yourself in the Café, the Relax Lounge, the Business Lounge, or the Sculpture Park, thanks to Rist and Martinez, St. Gallen's Bleicheli district will never be the same again.

Not all objects in the area got rubbered by Rist. Standing in contrast to all the red-covered objects, silver trashcans gleam in the sunlight (as all trash cans do in Switzerland). Trees and existing street signs were also spared. The water fountain, completely covered in red rubber, was not.

Suspended above the red lounge are 3-meter blimp-shaped lights that resemble giant potatoes or stones. These lights glow orange, red, blue, and violet in the evenings, giving the City Lounge a club-like atmosphere.

According to Raiffeisen, the bank that sponsored the design competition resulting in the *Stadtlounge*, the goal was to turn the soulless financial district into a public space where people lingered. It appears to have worked.

For more information:

The Stadtlounge is a five-minute walk from St. Gallen's main train station
Raffeisenplatz
St. Gallen
Always open
www.raiffeisen.ch/stadtlounge

38. Grill Sausages at 534 Fire Pits

There are 534 documented fire pits in Switzerland.

When this author first moved to Switzerland, she was not a sausage eater. She didn't eat hot dogs. She didn't eat corn dogs. She was not a consumer of pig products. This was a problem. When out and about in Switzerland, sometimes it's sausage or starvation. And the Cervelat, a name that comes from the Latin *cerebellum*, meaning brain (although pig and pork brain is no longer used in the modern Cervelat), is the most popular Swiss sausage.

Around 160 million Cervelats are consumed every year in Switzerland by a population of 8 million. This means the average Swiss eats around twenty to twenty-five Cervelats a year. The Cervelat, a mixture of about 25 percent beef and 75 percent pork, is made from 90 percent Swiss meat. The sausage is sometimes eaten raw, but the most popular way of cooking it is over an open fire.

At some point, if you're like this author, you may find yourself at a *Schweizer Familie Feuerstellen* (Swiss Family Fire Pit) with a stainless steel skewer trying to fit in by proudly grilling…a marshmallow. The thing is, your marshmallow will look weak and sad among all the meaty sausages surrounding it. Swiss kids will stare. They don't roast marshmallows.

But don't worry. Eventually, you'll be planning your grill outing on a Swiss mountaintop like a local. You'll cook your Cervelat over an open fire and eat it Swiss style, holding your sausage in one hand and your tube of mustard in the other.

But here's the thing. The grilling choices may be Cervelat or Cervelat (the Cervelat is the Swiss national sausage, after all), but when it comes to where you grill your Cervelat, there are over 500 fire pit options just waiting for you to find them using their GPS coordinates.

Yes, grilling a sausage in the woods is such an important thing to do in Switzerland that there is an entire website (and book) devoted to helping you find your ideal fire pit. Click on a canton, click on a pit, and you'll find its exact coordinates and altitude, along with the hiking route that will lead you to it. And don't forget to look at the accompanying fire pit photos so you can make sure your fire pit of choice is up to your standards. There's no point in wasting time with a pit that's less than perfect. After all, grilling a sausage is serious business in Switzerland. Especially if you want to time your treat for the correct lunch hour—noon.

If you're not a planner—in other words, if you aren't Swiss—your best bet for finding an on-the-fly fire pit is in canton Bern. At the time of writing, canton Bern had exactly 109 documented fire pits, more than any other canton. This does not mean that other cantons do not have many splendid places for grilling, but rather that their fire pits are unorganized and undocumented. And unorganized and undocumented will not a proper Swiss sausage experience make.

For more information:

Find Your Fire Pit on the Web:
www.schweizerfamilie.ch/wanderungen-ausfluege/#filter=223

Find Your Fire Pit in the Book:
Title: 534 Feuerstellen der Schweizer Familie
Publisher: Werd Verlag

39. Don't Bargain at the Flea Market

Finding unique items at a Swiss flea market is easy, but bargaining is not.

Nothing demonstrates your foreignness in Switzerland more than trying to bargain at a Swiss flea market. When a Swiss names his price, that is the price. If you feel the urge to argue about it, you're probably not Swiss enough yet.

If you consider Switzerland's second-hand scene, the country is clearly not a buyer's market. This can be good—if you're a seller. In fact, this author has sold used items in Switzerland for more than she paid for them new in the U.S.

Kind of makes her want to hop on a plane with a bunch of junk right now.

But she digresses. Over the years, this author frequented many Swiss second-hand markets. She was a regular at the Baden flea market, which takes place on the last Saturday of every month, and she never missed an opportunity to step into a *Brockenhaus*, or a second-hand store. She also occasionally visited Switzerland's online second-hand store, in other words, the eBay of Switzerland, which is, in independent Swiss style, not eBay.ch, but ricardo.ch.

All of these second-hand Swiss entities have a few things in common: the prices of things are high and most sellers are not willing to bargain.

And there, dear reader, lie both the challenge and the cultural experience. So this author encourages you to go to the next and nearest Swiss flea market and try to bargain. It's quite an amazing experience to find a man selling an old garden gnome who'd rather take it back to his garage than let you buy it for anything less than 50 SF.

But you may get lucky. This author once asked a flea market seller if she could have 5 SF off the total price for buying not one, but two old road signs. "Nein" was the reply from the seller, until the seller's daughter (was she foreign born?) reasoned with her mother behind the scenes and this author went home with two old signs and one big Swiss *Preishit*, the Swiss version of a great deal.

Nevertheless, this author would like to apologize ahead of time for those of you who may try to buy used belts at a Swiss flea market and find that they're not only out of your price range but also that the price for them is non-negotiable. Zurich, Geneva, and Bern weren't listed as the world's most expensive cities for nothing.

Just know there is hope. This author was once was able to bargain a seller down to 1 SF for a pair of used baby socks at a Swiss flea market—the things she goes through for her daughter! It wasn't easy, but then again, it's not easy to save money in Switzerland. And when you do it successfully, it's a real thrill.

Viel Spass, mitenand.

Recommended flea markets:

Bürkliplatz Flea Market (Zurich, every Saturday, May-October)

Baden Flea Market (Baden, last Saturday of every month, March-November)

Petersplatz Flea Market (Basel, every Saturday)

Plainpalais Flea Market (Geneva, every Wednesday & Saturday + first Sunday of every month)

Reussteg Flea Market (Lucerne, every Saturday, May-October)

40. Eat British Cheese in the Land of Gruyère

When people think of cheese in Switzerland they usually think of Gruyère, raclette, or Emmentaler. They do not usually think cheddar or Red Cheshire. But that's all changing thanks to Michael Jones, who runs the British Cheese Centre of Switzerland. Slowly but surely, he's turning Swiss cheese lovers into British cheese connoisseurs.

What started as an online venture selling British cheese to expats in Switzerland has become so successful that it's turned into a permanent shop that focuses on farmhouse cheeses from small British dairies. The number of loyal Swiss customers is growing and the majority of Jones' customers are now Swiss. Some Swiss families are so taken with the novel idea that the Brits care as much about cheese as they do that they shell out 300 SF for a selection of British cheeses to go. (Jones can't imagine a British family ever spending that much on a bag of cheese.)

British cheese has grown so popular in Switzerland that it's become normal for 17,000 kilos of British cheese to make its way to Jones' shop every year. If you want to be a little more Swiss, you need to eat a little Godminster organic cheddar or Scottish fondue too. Depending on your luck, the British Cheese Centre of Switzerland will have between 30 and 70 varieties of cheese to offer you. In fact, according to Jones, Britain makes more cheese than Switzerland and France combined. While no better or worse than Swiss cheese, Jones believes the taste of British cheese is more distinctive due to the fact that Britain is an island.

Need another reason to visit the British Cheese Centre of Switzerland? It's located in Zurich's first indoor market, Im Viadukt, which is worthy of a visit in itself, British cheese or not. Unlike most Swiss renovation projects, which polish the already shiny, the Im Viadukt endeavor transformed a 19th century railway viaduct into a usable cultural and commercial attraction.

Once deserted, Zurich's fifth district around Hardbrücke is now a whir of shoppers buying gifts at independently owned boutiques, diners lingering at restaurants and cafés, and locals discovering why cheddar is worth eating—even in the land of Emmentaler.

For more information:

The British Cheese Centre
Markthalle Im Viadukt
Limmatstrasse 231
8005 Zurich
www.britishcheese.ch

41. Read *A Bell for Ursli* and Hike the Story

An example of sgraffito, a plaster carving technique unique to the Engadine Valley.

It's not often that a beautiful children's story can turn into an equally breathtaking day out. But this is Switzerland, and anything is possible when you're hiking here—even reading to your children. Which brings us to Guarda, where you can hike in a storybook setting while pages from one of the most famous Swiss children's tales unfold along your route.

Schellen-Ursli (*A Bell for Ursli*), by Alois Carigiet and Selina Chönz, tells the tale of a little boy who lives in Guarda. To find a cowbell big enough to allow him to lead the spring parade, he hikes alone to his family's chalet high up above Guarda. And there's a trail that will take you along his supposed route.

While the not-so-Swiss might imagine that a hike involving a children's book would also be child-friendly, it's important to note that this is not the case. The *Schellen-Ursli-Weg* is not stroller-friendly, nor is it easy for young children as parts of it are quite steep, especially the first section leading up from the village of Guarda. But it's enchanting for older children and adults who enjoy fairy-tale views, as well as for parents who don't mind carrying small children up the mountain.

The 6-kilometer path, which takes between two and four hours to hike depending on your nationality, begins in the village of Guarda (follow the signs with the illustration of Ursli on them). Rising above the village, the path offers amazing views of the town, the Tuoi Valley, and the Piz Buin. Cows and meadows greet you along the way, as do the pages of the story, which is told in both English and German on trail signs. There are also games related to the story for the children to play. Other highlights include streams, a lake, several fire pits, and of course, Ursli's family chalet. The circular route is usually accessible from mid-May through mid-October.

Once back in Guarda, which is one of the area's oldest villages, be sure to admire the *sgraffito*-decorated houses. *Sgraffito* is a style of craftsmanship unique to the Engadine Valley, in which a newly applied layer of plaster is carved to reveal the gray plaster underneath, creating timeless designs on the facades of buildings and houses.

The Hotel Meisser & Restaurant, which has been around since 1893, is an atmospheric location for a post-hike drink or meal. In fact, the hotel is so picturesque it's hard not to want to hug it. There are blue shutters, red geraniums, and a heart painted on the building above the rounded door. Not to mention the huge outdoor area for dining with views across the valley. The food is Swiss-priced, meaning entrées are around 25 SF or higher, but the food is well above average. Think white asparagus with ham and new potatoes, summer salad with salmon and goat cheese, and freshly made berry lemonade.

From Guarda, another nice (and easier) trail leads to the traditional Romansh-speaking village of Ardez, where you can admire some of the area's most decorative houses. Then from Ardez, why not take a short train ride to Scuol and soothe your sore muscles in the town's famous spa, Bogn Engiadina Scuol?

For more information:

    Schellen-Ursli-Weg
    Start: Guarda, cumün
    Finish: Guarda, cumün
    Route: Guarda Dorf – Charal – Platuns – Lajet – Clüs – Perlas – Valatscha – Plan Champatsch – Plan da Pors – Prasüras – Er da Teja – Praders – Guarda Dorf
    Length: 6.2 kilometers.
    Hiking Time: 2 hours, 7 minutes (To be exact)
    Altitude change: + 316 m – 316 m
    Level of difficultly: Medium (Translation: Challenging for non-Swiss)
    Best time of year: Mid-May–Mid-October

    www.graubuenden.ch

42. Bathe in a Brewery. Or a Church.

The Mineralbad & Spa Samedan is Switzerland's first vertically built spa.

For over 2,000 years, the Swiss have been putting the country's abundant thermal springs to good use. You might as well take advantage of this history. The Swiss love the concept of *wellness*, the *Swinglish* word for relaxing spa experiences, so they constantly reimagine it. Many of the newest spas are designed by famous architects such as Peter Zumthor.

One of the oldest public spas to get overhauled is in the medieval spa town of Baden. The name of the town means, "to bathe"; in this small village alone, there are eighteen sulfurous springs, and they've been used since Roman times. How to find them? One way is to simply go for a walk along the Limmat River. Near the Limmathof Hotel, you'll run right into a steaming footbath, located along the river near the original hot spring. In mid-walk, you can simply take off your shoes and socks, sit on a bench, and enjoy a soothing, steaming soak. For free.

Many towns in Switzerland, including Baden, were built around their natural hot springs and therefore have wonderful wellness opportunities. In Bad Ragaz, Bad Zurzach, Schinznach Bad, Scuol, Leukerbad, and many others, public spas offer an amazing Swiss spa experience for an equally amazing value. Often you can relax for several hours for less than the price of a dinner entrée. Spa experiences are so popular in Switzerland that one company, Aqua Spa Resorts, is making an entire business out of reinventing wellness, allowing those in the know (who are also willing to spend a bit more than the price of admission to a public spa) the opportunity to enjoy their mineral spa experience in former breweries, landmark churches, and other breathtaking locations. In the process, the company is transforming the very nature of relaxation.

At the Zurich Thermalbad & Spa, you can bathe within the hundred-year-old vaulted stone walls of the former Hürlimann Brewery. From there, you can retire to the rooftop pool to watch the sun set over Zurich. If this doesn't feel spiritual enough, you can go to Samedan, a town in the Engadine Valley, and bathe in a church. The Mineralbad & Spa Samedan is located right in the center of town. Just look for the town's church, and you'll find Switzerland's first vertically built spa. As you ascend from one pool to the next, you'll end up bathing on four different levels and in varying degrees of water, including the highlight: a rooftop pool under the church tower complete with a view of the Alps—a divine place to contemplate just how close to heaven you are.

You can get your spa kicks in many Swiss hotels too. Allow me to count the ways. There's Peter Zumthor's modern spa masterpiece at the Hotel Therme in Vals. There's the cool blue and grey mosaic-covered walls surrounding the warm waters at the Edec Roc hotel in Ascona. And there's the light-filled mountain spa at the Tschuggen Bergoase, designed by Mario Botta.

Let it be known that this author has done her spa homework—which, admittedly, wasn't unpleasant. Her conclusion? It's hard to go wrong with a Swiss spa. But if you're going just for the healing waters, go to Baden's Thermalbad, whose water has the highest mineral concentration in Switzerland (its new spa, also designed by Mario Botta, will open in 2018). But if you're going for pure aesthetics, head to Locarno. At the Termali Salini & Spa Locarno, you can bathe in warm salt water while you sit in a bubble chair and look out at Lake Maggiore and the Alps. Thanks to its infinity pool design, it looks as if you're lounging in the lake. You'll find it hard to leave—but that's why they have this little thing called closing time.

43. Go to Liechtenstein (Because You Can)

There is one very important reason to go to Liechtenstein: to say you've been to Liechtenstein. It's a feather-in-the-cap for anyone who lives by bucket lists, and since this author does, of course she will encourage you to visit a country only 160-square-kilometers small if it will eliminate a larger-than-life item from your list.

It's not that the fourth-smallest state in Europe isn't worthy—it's just that it's not much different from many places in Switzerland. Liechtenstein uses the Swiss franc, you can ride on its buses using your Swiss Travel Pass, and its residents speak a German dialect. If you don't pay close attention, you'll miss the fact that you're no longer in Switzerland. So if you do make the extra effort to go to Liechtenstein, it feels like there should be more of a reward than Alpine vistas, financial experts, and expensive hotels. Unfortunately, Vaduz's main drag is a bit of a letdown—despite being crowned by a 700-year-old castle. But since Hans-Adam II, the Prince of Liechtenstein, still lives there, the best part of Liechtenstein isn't accessible to tourists—even those who are traveling like locals.

That said, if you find yourself realizing you've crossed the border into Liechtenstein, congratulations. Here are a few things you could do:

1. Buy a postage stamp and/or visit the free stamp museum in Vaduz (basically one big room with stamps on the walls—welcome to the exciting place that is Liechtenstein!)

2. Get a passport stamp from the Liechtenstein Center (fancy name for the tourist office in Vaduz). This is a privilege you must pay for, however. A stamp in your passport costs about 3 SF. Worth it? Of course.

3. Take a picture of yourself at the border with one foot in Switzerland and one in Liechtenstein. This is free.

Gotten your thrill out of Liechtenstein yet? No? Then try touring Liechtenstein by bicycle. This may be the best way to see the country for four reasons:

1. Crossing the border is more fun by bike.
2. Taking that border foot photo (see above) is easier by bike.
3. The scenic bike route from Sargans, Switzerland to Vaduz follows the Rhine River.
4. You can easily bike across Liechtenstein in a day and be rewarded with an extreme feeling of accomplishment.

So. If you're feeling sporty and motivated, here's this author's way to make the most out of that almost obligatory visit to Liechtenstein:

1. Bike from Sargans, Switzerland to Vaduz, Liechtenstein along the turquoise Rhine. Bikes can be rented at the Sargans train station if you don't have your own. From Vaduz, you can head back the same way via bike or bus or continue your ride to Buchs. Veloland.ch also recommends an easy 45-kilometer round-trip route starting in Buchs that includes the Sargans-Vaduz section. They call this route the Fünf Schlössertour (Five Castle Route). It is route Nr. 555. www.veloland.ch/en/routes/route-0555.html

OR

2. Coordinate your visit to Liechtenstein with a slowUp bike ride (see Idea 11) since this will include a little bit of Liechtenstein and a lot of free granola bars. The slowUp ride to Liechtenstein usually takes place every May.

For more information:

www.liechtenstein.li

www.slowup.ch

www.veloland.ch

44. See Why the Swiss Riviera Deserves its Name

Victor Hugo wrote this about Lausanne in his book *The Rhine*: "I saw the lake over the roofs, the mountains over the lake, clouds over the mountains, and stars over the clouds. It was like a staircase where my thoughts climbed step by step and broadened at each new height."

The Swiss Riviera, a 32-kilometer stretch along Lac Léman (Lake Geneva) from Chateau de Chillon to Lausanne, has inspired many. Lord Byron, Alexandre Dumas, and Charles Dickens to name but three. One of the most breathtaking areas in this region is the Lavaux. Here, 830 hectares of terraced vineyards clinging to Lake Geneva transform from green to gold every October, gilding the region's already golden reputation.

To experience the best of Switzerland's largest contiguous vineyard region the Swiss way, begin a three-hour wine hike in St-Saphorin, a medieval village where the perfume of fermenting grapes fills the air. Don't forget to admire the church—its steeple is famous for gracing wine bottles. Souvenir, anyone?

From St-Saphorin, it's over 11 kilometers to the end of the hike in Lutry, so you might as well give in to your thirst and have a glass of wine along your route through this UNESCO World Heritage Site. This trail is wide and paved, making it a great option for strollers and families, as well as for those who can't pass by a wine cellar without stopping for a taste.

As you walk, you'll probably have a lot of questions: Should I look at the vineyards, whose terraces can be traced back to the 11th century? Look at Lake Geneva? Look at the Alps? Look at the golden train humming by? Look at my life and wish I was living it here? It can be hard to decide what to look at. The Swiss Riviera is like that. It almost feels too beautiful to be real—a theme played out in most of Switzerland—but here this theme crescendos to a double forte.

It doesn't hurt that the Swiss Riviera is also home to Switzerland's largest concentration of Michelin-starred restaurants, fairy-tale castles like Chateau de Chillon and Chateau de Aigle, and the world-famous Montreux Jazz Festival. If you visit the area in the springtime and you like treasure hunts, you might enjoy searching for the narcissus fields near Caux (see Idea 4).

Swiss Wine Hike through the Lavaux Vineyards
Starting Point: St-Saphorin (train accessible)
Ending Point: Lutry (train accessible)
11.7 km, 3 hours, 15 minutes
Best times: March through October

Wines from the region to try:
Chasselas, Gamay, and Pinot Noir

Chateau de Chillon
(*Achtung*—this is the most visited monument in Switzerland)
Avenue de Chillon 21
1820 Veytaux
www.chillon.ch

Chateau de Aigle
Place du Château 1
1860 Aigle
www.chateauaigle.ch

45. Drink to Swiss Wine Being Rarely Exported

There are several vineyards above Wettingen.

This author has a French friend who lives in Switzerland. She'll call him Jean-Claude for the purposes of this book. Jean-Claude really loves wine. He can't help it. He's from Burgundy.

Jean-Claude collects international wines, regardless of border limitations. His idea of a vacation is to go vineyard hopping and wine shopping. He has over 800 bottles of wine in his wine cellar in Ehrendingen. You don't eat dinner at his house without a proper wine for every course.

You could say Jean-Claude is a wine snob. It's not exactly Pommard wine or nothing, but unlike this author, he's not going to show up at The Picnic Etude in Baden (see Idea 12) with plastic cups and a Robert Mondavi. He pimps his picnic with proper wine glasses and wine courses—even when he knows he'll be dining *al fresco* with this author's daughter, who uses a picnic blanket like a dance floor.

Toddler at his picnic or not, "plastic cup" is not in Jean-Claude's vocabulary. But surprisingly, "Swiss wine" is. Despite having 14,835 hectares of vineyards and growing grapes since Roman times, Switzerland does not have much of a reputation for wine. This is mainly because unlike cheese and chocolate, most Swiss wine is not exported. In fact, only about 1.7 percent of Swiss wine finds its way across the border—but this could be changing. In an effort to promote Swiss wine, the Swiss foreign ministry now pays for the cost of its transport to embassies abroad.

But if you're not a diplomat, drink your Swiss wine while you're in Switzerland. Where will you find the good stuff? Cortis specializes in Swiss wines and you can order from them online. There is also a start-up in Geneva called Wiine.me. And of course, grocery stores like Coop and Denner also carry a variety of Swiss wines.

Here are some Swiss wines to try:

> Sottobosco, Rosso del Ticino 2010 (By far this author's absolute favorite Swiss wine. The vineyard is practically in Italy.) www.agriloro.ch

> Gewürztraminer, Svizzera Italiana 2011 (Fresh and dry) www.agriloro.ch

> Assemblage Rouge Reserve Hurlevent, Les Fils de Charles Favre, AOC Valais 2011 (Usually available at Coop and Manor.) www.favre-vins.ch

> Pinot Noir 3 & 4, 2011 from Schlossgut Bachtobel in Thurgau, where vines have been grown for eight generations. www.bachtobel.ch

> Wines produced by Weingut Pircher in Eglisau, a vineyard on the banks of the Rhine. www.weingut-pircher.ch

When you're ready to celebrate your introduction to Swiss wine, make sure to uphold the Swiss tradition of saying *Prost* if you're in the German-speaking area. To toast each person you are drinking with, look them in the eye as you clink glasses with them while saying *Prost* + Name of Person you are toasting. Not saying their name is considered rude.

46. Lounge by Lake Cauma and the Swiss Grand Canyon

Grüezi mitenand, and welcome to Idea 46. For the next two days, we'll be in Flims. Maybe you've heard of it. Together with Laax, it's a famous ski resort that's worth visiting at any time of year. There are turquoise lakes. Mountain rivers. And the "oh my gosh look at that" Rhine Gorge, otherwise known as the Swiss Grand Canyon.

Here's an itinerary that will take you deep into this area of Graubünden.

Day 1: Take the train to Chur, Switzerland's oldest city. Then take the PostBus to the Caumasee stop. From here, it's a short fifteen-minute hike down to the Cauma Lake. Chill out on a lounge chair, dive into this sparkling turquoise jewel of a lake, rent a paddleboat (about 15 SF/hour), eat lunch at its restaurant (late May to October), or just flirt with a few locals. Graubünden, according to my Swiss friend Silvia, is the canton where the Swiss German speakers have the sexiest accents.

Follow this with an easy forty-minute hike to Restaurant Conn on the Senda Ruinaulta, or the Swiss Rhine Gorge Route. Five minutes beyond Conn, you'll find the "Il Spir" viewing platform. Up here, 12.5 meters above the hiking path and over 396 meters above the Anterior Rhine (Vorderrhein), you'll have 180-degree views of the Swiss Grand Canyon. You can thank a prehistoric rockslide for this collection of bizarre rock formations. Say your superlatives, click your camera, and stroll back to Waldhaus/Flims along the orchid-strewn canyon landscapes. Dinner and a drink are waiting for you at Surselva Bräu, a small local brewery with a great restaurant and even better beer.

Flims – Caumasee – Conn: 3.6 kilometers, 55 minutes, altitude change 150 meters

Day 2: Take the cable car from Flims to Naraus (around 24 SF one way or 30 SF round trip) and hike to the Segneshütte. This is a panoramic hike of medium difficulty, and you'll enjoy spectacular landscapes, a refreshing waterfall, and a mountain river before heading back down, either via the cable car from Naraus, or if you're there from July-October, you can take the bus back from Alp Nagens. (Make sure to check the bus schedule, it doesn't run every day.)

Naraus – Segneshütte – Alp Nagens: 5.5 kilometers, 2 hours, altitude change 300 meters

Other ideas:

Raft down the river. The Anterior Rhine is a popular place to paddle and raft for beginners, especially from Ilanz to Reichenau. www.swissraft.ch

Hike the round-trip Rhine Gorge Route (Senda Ruinaulta—see Day 1 ideas) www.myswitzerland.com/en/interests/hiking/senda-ruinaulta-the-swiss-rhine-gorge-route.html

The Alpabzug (cow parade) takes place every fall in Flims. Check the Flims website for the date, get up early, and watch the cows come home. See Idea 9.

Where to stay:

Hotel des Alpes in Waldhaus/Flims (right near the Caumasee bus stop and minutes from the turquoise Cauma Lake.) About 200 SF/night for a double, including breakfast. The large rooms include soap. Yes, free soap! Go ahead, celebrate. www.hoteldesalpes.ch

Where to eat:

Surselva Bräu

A fun brewery that let me order both a beer and a *Kinderschnitzel*. What's not to like? You could also try a *Brezel*, or freshly baked pretzel, along with cream of beer soup.

Rudi Dadens 3
7018 Flims Waldhaus
www.surselva-bier.ch

Note:

To save money, why not use Reka checks? The Hotel des Alpes will let you pay for half your room with these checks and the cable car people in Flims take them too. Many Swiss companies offer the chance for their employees to purchase Reka checks every year at a discount of 20 percent. You can also purchase them at Coop grocery stores, Manor department stores, and Jumbo, although here the discount is only 3 percent. Over 9,000 Swiss hotels, restaurants, and museums accept Reka checks, and they can also be used to pay for Swiss public transport. There is a Reka Guide, available online or via the Reka-Guide App, that details which places accept Reka. www.reka.ch

47. Discover Why Swiss Cheese has Holes

The famous cheese holes happen here.

In North America, Switzerland's most exported cheese is simply called, "Swiss cheese," as if Switzerland were the land of only one cheese instead of 450. In any case, Emmentaler, the Swiss name for "Swiss cheese," is a holey cheese that's been around since the Middle Ages. It comes from an area known as the Emmental.

The Emmental, located in the heart of Switzerland to the west of Lucerne, has very little urban development. Instead, it has rolling landscapes. It has people who say *Grüezi* in possibly the cutest accent in Switzerland (sounds like "Grüessech"). And it has cows. Why no one goes to Emmental—except to visit its cheese dairy—is beyond this author.

So go west, young reader. Spend a day that's one part traditional Swiss hiking and one part traditional Swiss tourism. First, walk through the wonderful hills and valleys of the Emmental. Then visit the dairy that put the holes in the cheese most English-speakers call Swiss.

Your 3.5-kilometer, hour-long Swiss hike begins in the middle of nowhere and ends at the biggest attraction in the area—the cheese dairy. Start by taking a train to Burgdorf (a village worth seeing in its own right), and then a bus to Lueg (Bus 468), where your hike of easy-medium difficulty begins.

In Lueg, follow the yellow hiking signs (and the sound of cowbells) to Junkholz while admiring the patchwork patterns of the grassy hills and the curvy roads leading to geranium-decked farmhouses. If it's a clear day, you will also have views of the Eiger, Mönch, and Jungfrau. After Junkholz, you'll pass the village of Schnabel, finally ending your hike in Affoltern i.E. at the Emmentaler-Schaukäserei (a cheese—and admittedly somewhat cheesy—dairy).

This cheese hub is not as extensive as the more popular cheese dairy in Gruyère, but it's also not as crowded. There's a wonderful picnic area, a playground to keep kids (or adults acting like kids) busy, a cheese shop, a restaurant serving everything from cheese crème soup to fondue and raclette, and possibly the oldest cheese making house in the world that can still live up to modern Swiss standards of cleanliness.

At the cheese dairy, you can watch as 1200 liters of milk are turned into one mold of Emmentaler. First, the milk is stirred in a giant vat and heated to over 50 degrees Celsius. Once it curdles and coagulates, it's poured into round molds where any remaining liquid is pressed out. The cheese is then submerged in salt water for a few days before going into a storage room to ferment and ripen for at least four months. As it ripens, lactose bacteria produce carbon dioxide bubbles in the still soft curd. The airtight rind means the carbon dioxide bubbles cannot escape—so when the cheese solidifies, the bubbles remain, leaving behind the famous holes. Aren't bacteria wonderful?

From the Schaukäserei, you can return to Burgdorf from the bus stop "Affoltern i.E. Dorf" via Bus 471.

For more information:

>Emmentaler Schaukäserei
>Schaukäsereistrasse 6
>3416 Affoltern im Emmental
>www.emmentaler-schaukaeserei.ch
>www.bls.ch (bus website with hiking tips)

Hike:

>Lueg – Junkholz – Affoltern i.E.
>3.5 kilometers, 1 hour
>Easy-Medium
>Altitude Difference: 100 meters
>Recommended Time of Year: April–October
>Stroller Friendly: Yes

48. Relax for Exactly One Minute

The Swiss like to take morning and afternoon breaks. But they do not just take a timeout when the spirit moves them. Their breaks are like the Swiss themselves—scheduled. The Swiss are early risers, and by nine o'clock they need a rest. In the Swiss German-speaking area of Switzerland, they take their first break at exactly 9 a.m. This *Pause* is called a z'Nüni, based on the German word for "nine." Their second break is exactly at 4 p.m. It's called a "z'Vieri," based on—you guessed it—the German word for "four."

You can (and should) take a z'Nüni if you would like to be a little more local. When the clock strikes nine, immediately put a *Gipfeli* (the Swiss German version of a croissant with a crisper crust and a less buttery taste) in one hand and a coffee in the other, and you'll be well on your way to becoming culturally appropriate.

If you want to get fancy and you're in Zurich, have your z'Nüni at Café Conditorei Schober. Housed in a 13th century building, this pastry shop and café is now called Péclard after its owner, Michel Péclard. Inspired by the décor and delicacies of Paris, this Swiss tea salon and boutique coffeehouse may remind those who frequent these kinds of places a little too often (such as this author) of Ladurée in Paris.

Péclard is famous for its hot chocolate and its sophisticated variety of dining options. Each room in the café has a different style, so be sure to take a stroll before you decide on the ideal atmosphere for your mood. Red velvet chairs and chandeliers? Plants and handcrafted Zuber wallpaper from Alsace? Breezes and cobblestones?

Sweets are also sold "to go" in the original 19th century candy shop. There are Parisian macarons in almost every color of the rainbow and so many pastries you could spend a month of z'Nünis trying them all. Come to think of it, why not do just that?

For more information:

Conditorei Péclard im Schober
Napfgasse 4
8001 Zurich
+41 (0)44 251 51 50
www.peclard-zurich.ch

49. Border Shop

For a slice of Swiss culture (and some good deals) there is one place you should go: outside Switzerland. In border towns like Constance, Germany and Bregenz, Austria, you'll see parking lots filled with hundreds of cars bearing Swiss license plates. The Interest Group of Swiss Retail Trade estimated that Swiss shoppers drove 720 million miles to border shop in 2013, spending almost 10 billion SF abroad in the process.

And can you blame them? The Consumer Protection Foundation shows that the Swiss pay 15 billion SF ($15.8 billion) more for household goods than their neighbors in bordering countries. And for the Swiss, crossing a border is so easy it's almost a fact of life. Almost 50 percent of Swiss people live closer than 65 kilometers to a border.

So crossing the borders the Swiss are—and if you want to be more Swiss, you need to join them. There were so many Swiss driving across the border from Basel to Germany every day that the city built a new tram line (Tram 8) to cut down on traffic. Constance has opened a new 500-space parking lot for its Swiss shoppers. And by 2017, Bregenz will have opened a new shopping center for a certain little demographic with an enormous purchasing power. (A 2015 UBS study showed the inhabitants of Zurich and Geneva have the second and third highest purchasing power in the world (behind the residents of Luxembourg)).

It's crazy to see it, but across the border Swiss chocolate, Swiss cheese, and many Swiss products are cheaper than they are in Switzerland. Even something as basic as a bag of tortilla chips can cost 75 percent less across the border. But the truth is, many of these border towns are better used not just for their deals but also for their local specialties and charm. This author wants to make sure you don't miss some of her favorites, so she's listed them below.

While some border towns will accept Swiss francs, you will not get a favorable exchange rate by using them. So if you go, be sure to have Euros handy. The best way to obtain Euros is to withdraw them from an ATM in the border country upon arrival. Residents of Switzerland with a Swiss banking account can withdraw Euros from Swiss ATM machines as well, although usually the bills are only available in denominations of 50 and 100—not useful in countries like Germany, France, and Austria, where smaller bills are preferred.

Border Shopping Towns to Experience:

Town: Waldshut, Germany
How: Direct train from Baden, Switzerland
When: Saturdays for the market in the old town
Must try: Nussstollen (sweet nut bread) from Bäckerei Wehrle (Kaiserstrasse 63)
Must do: Stroll the geranium-filled old town

Town: Constance, Germany
How: Direct train from Zurich
When: Outdoor markets on Tuesdays, Wednesdays, Fridays, and Saturdays
Must try: Ruppaner Bier (the local beer)
Must do: Walk around the colorful harbor

Town: Evian-les-Bains, France
How: Ferry from Lausanne-Ouchy (20 minutes)
When: Market days are Tuesdays and Fridays
Must try: Savoyard cheese from the market
Must do: Visit the Cachat Spring, the most famous of the natural sources of Evian water

Town: Feldkirch, Austria
How: Train from Buchs SG

When: Market days are Tuesdays and Saturdays
Must try: Austria's largest schnitzels at Schattenburg Castle (Burggasse 1)
Must do: Visit the 13th century Schattenburg Castle for views over Feldkirch

50. Hike on Slippery History

The larch trees near the Morteratsch Glacier turn yellow and gold in October.

If this author had to choose her favorite hike in Switzerland, it would probably be the Morteratsch Glacier hike—especially if it's mid-October. There are several reasons for this.

One is the sheer beauty of orange and yellow larch trees framing the icy snow and the (hopefully) blue sky. The Engadine area is famous for its autumn colors, and not without reason.

Two is the length (approx. 5-6 kilometers, 1 hour 40 minutes total) and ease of the walk (fairly flat, on a mostly wide and graveled path), which allows one to admire the scenery without being distracted by blisters or aching muscles.

Three is easy access. The hike begins and ends at the Morteratsch train station, whose neighbor is the Hotel Restaurant Morteratsch—a relaxing place for lunch.

And the fourth reason this author loves the Morteratsch

Glacier hike? It tells a powerful story—even if it's a sad one. Only about 120 years ago, the Morteratsch Glacier stretched almost two kilometers further into the valley. The hiking trail follows the former path of the glacier, and the signs along the route demonstrate just how far the glacier has retreated since 1878.

Still, there's nothing like hiking an environmental tragedy to understand the true impact of it. Global warming skeptics are particularly invited. It's hard to say global warming is a myth when you're walking in its path.

In summary, the Morteratsch Glacier hike, which is about three kilometers to the glacier and three kilometers back on the same trail, has a reward at both ends. The way there leads you to the Morteratsch Glacier, while giving you a powerful lesson. And the way back leads you to Hotel Restaurant Morteratsch and pumpkin ravioli.

If you visit in the winter, you won't be treated to the autumn colors, but that's okay—you'll get a trail that doubles as a cross-country ski track (classic and skating) instead. Things could be worse.

For more information:

> You can extend the hike by starting and/or ending in Pontresina.
> www.pontresina.ch

> The trail (including the Pontresina extension) is stroller-accessible.

> The Bernina Railway Line from St. Moritz to Tirano, Italy, stops in Morteratsch (and in Pontresina).
> www.rhb.ch

Hotel Restaurant Morteratsch
www.morteratsch.ch

You can easily combine this trip with other local ideas in this book over a long weekend in the area. Ideas 94, 95, and 99 are on the same train line.

51. Walk in the Snowy, Candlelit Woods

Warm up for your walk with a little aerobics.

A thousand candles. Five kilometers. One unforgettable walk in the woods. That's what Grieder Sport's Silvester Walking & Nordic Walking event has to offer. The tradition to hike in the candlelight began in Baden in 2003 and has taken place every December (or early January) since then.

Before the event begins, look for a warm-up aerobics session, complete with strobe lights and people wearing tracksuits. *Grüezi*, 1980. Needless to say, witnessing (or participating) in the warm-up session is an unforgettable experience and worth the price of entry alone. Then, as super organized as only the Swiss can be, you'll be sent out in groups to hike in the Baldegg woods above Baden. The trails will be dotted by flickering candles, which are placed precisely at regular intervals.

Don't be like this author, though, and expect a stroll in the woods. The Swiss are serious about walking and doing it in the dark doesn't change this. Most sprint the trail as if the event were a competition instead of an atmospheric experience. Despite being overtaken by Swiss children, this author enjoyed the experience—especially since it included a warm restaurant meal afterwards.

Reservations (and walking sticks) are recommended for the event. Because a restaurant meal is included, the number of participants is limited and by now you should know that the Swiss love walking—so register early.

Typically the meal (usually pasta) is held at either Restaurant Belvédère Baden or Restaurant Baldegg. The walk usually starts and ends at the restaurant. Bus 5 from Baden's main train station towards Baldegg will take you to either starting place.

For more information:

Silvester Walking & Nordic Walking
Register with Grieder Sport (event sponsor)
Cost: approximately SF 40

Grieder Sport
Mellingerstrasse 1
5400 Baden
www.griedersport.ch (only in German)

RVBW
Baden Bus Routes & Timetables
(You'll want Bus 5, direction Baldegg)
www.rvbw.ch

52. Celebrate Static Electricity

Gigantic bubble making is just one of the activities that makes science fun.

Technorama, Switzerland's Winterthur-based science museum, has something for everyone: drums, electric trains, gigantic bubble making, and—the real feature—taking a picture of yourself under the influence of static electricity.

At Technorama, you learn by experimentation. Touching and trying are both encouraged. There are over 500 exhibits spread across three floors (a huge museum by Swiss standards) to explore. And there's a bonus for those still learning one of the four official Swiss languages—there are English translations available for almost everything too. The museum receives over 250 million visitors a year.

Ready to join the crowds? Then pick up a pencil and sharpen your mind. Send wooden balls down wooden rods. Or make a connection between theoretical physics and everyday experiences. Technorama will redefine what you think of electricity, magnetism, and math. But most of all, it will prove that science can be fun.

And speaking of fun, the museum's basement features one of the world's best toy train collections (would you expect anything less of the Swiss?). Whether you imagine yourself playing with them or you appreciate the technical and historic portrait of rail transportation development they offer, the trains are something for both the young and the young at heart.

Since Technorama is a Swiss museum, the outdoors is a part of it too. The museum's park is not only a wonderful place for a picnic (naturally, there are barbeque sites, and the ticket office has charcoal if you've stupidly forgotten to bring your own) but it's also a place to learn about sun, wind, and water.

Naturally, time is as important here as it is everywhere in Switzerland, so four sundials teach you to read time depending on the sun's position so you are prepared in the .001 percent chance your Swiss watch should ever fail you. There's a wind machine too if you want to experience hurricane-like conditions or, if you prefer, you could make a garden hose dance instead.

For more information:

Technorama
Swiss Science Center
Technoramastrasse 1
8404 Winterthur
www.technorama.ch

Tip:

When traveling to Technorama by public transport, be sure to get the RailAway offer, which will save you 10 percent on both the entrance fee and the transport there. They also accept payment in Reka.
www.railaway.ch
www.reka.ch

53. Watch Hot Air Balloons Sway to Yodeling

Toggenburg is located in canton St. Gallen.

Now that you're more than halfway through this book, maybe you've noticed a trend—there are a lot of cool things to do in Switzerland. Especially if you think cool involves a combination of cows, hiking, and Alpine music. You're still reading, so congratulations, you must be the kind of person that gets up early to watch cows come down a mountain. To celebrate, let's discuss something that combines the best of Swiss cool: the International Ballooning Days Toggenburg.

Toggenburg, located in canton St. Gallen, is an area much like many others in Switzerland: it consists of hills, mountains, pastures, and Alpine meadows. What sets it apart is its accessibility from Zurich (about an hour east), its focus on traditional music (the area is home to a *Klangweg*, an entire hiking trail built around music and sound-making—ideal for children), and of course, its balloon festival.

International Ballooning Days Toggenburg (possibly the smallest take on "international" you'll ever experience) takes place on odd numbered years (2017, 2019, etc.) over an autumn weekend, and includes hot air balloon launches, entertainment, food and drinks, live music, and a children's afternoon featuring things like balloon cookie decorating, face painting, and a balloon candy drop.

The highlight of the festival is the Night Glow, where at least a dozen hot air balloons are placed along a lake to perform a light show coordinated with music. In 45 minutes, you'll likely watch the balloons glow to everything from yodeling to *The Circle of Life* from Disney's *Lion King*. Oh, and Johann Strauss and a random cowbell here and there will make appearances too. Trust this author when she says that the combination of music alone will be an experience in itself. Add the glowing balloons and you can reflect a bit more on the kind of cool worth going to the middle of nowhere for.

Anyway, a lot of people think that balloons that glow to both yodeling and Broadway themes in the middle of nowhere are cool, so make sure to get there at least an hour and a half ahead of time if you want a prime viewing spot along the lake.

For more information:

Ballontage Toggenburg
Ebnat-Kappel SG
Autumn, during odd years (2017, 2019)
Admission is free
www.ballontage.ch

54. Bike to the Top (and the End) of the World

Can a place feel like both the end of the world and the top of it at the same time? Bike up to Fusio at the end of the Lavizzara Valley and you'll experience a place as high as it is remote. The best part? Along the way you'll climb 846 meters on narrow switchback roads, going slowly enough to enjoy the views but breathing easily enough to snap a photo as you ride. Click. This author's vote is in: e-bikes, or bicycles with integrated electric motors that retain the ability to be pedaled by the rider, are a great way to see Switzerland (and can be easily rented at many Swiss train stations).

To get to the starting point of this recommended e-bike route, rent an e-bike from Locarno train station (you might want to reserve one ahead of time as the number of rentals are limited) and then go by bike (if you have time and a spare battery), bus (check first if they will take your e-bike on board), or private car from Locarno into the Maggia Valley. Bignasco, which is the last village before the valley splits into Val Bavona and Val Lavizzara, is where you'll officially begin your ride. Obviously, you could bike into either valley, but this author recommends the Val Lavizzara route, which will take you all the way from Bignasco to Fusio (and back) for an amazing 40-kilometer off-the-beaten-path-yet-on-the-road-ride.

Highlights of the Val Lavizzara route (which you can also enjoy totally by bus) include laundry clinging to crumbling 17th century buildings, a mid-ride lunch break at a traditional grotto, and a visit to the village of Mogno, with its must-see graphic masterpiece *Chiesa di San Giovanni Battista*, which was built in 1994 by Mario Botta (who also designed the San Francisco Museum of Modern Art). This church is a highlight, since it's possibly the only modern thing you'll see along the entire route, with the exception of the one-tank gas station in Broglio.

Grotto Pozzasc, in Peccia, is an atmospheric and convenient

mid-ride point to have lunch. The kitchen (and the small dining room) is in an old mill complete with geraniums spilling out the window. But the best place to sit is outside at one of the granite tables right next to the river. Here you'll have no choice but to enjoy a typically Ticinese lunch. The menu is small; options typically include homemade polenta, local cheeses, sausages, soup, and trout.

The best part of touring the Val Lavizzara on an e-bike is the ability to hop on and off at will. There are so many villages, cows, and camera-worthy sights along the way that it's beyond the scope of this book to name them all. But in the end, that's a good thing. Because sometimes the best discoveries in travel are the ones you make yourself.

For more information:

Rent a Bike
www.rentabike.ch

Locarno Stazione FFS
Piazza Stazione
6600 Locarno

Grotto Pozzasc
6694 Peccia
www.pozzasc.ch

55. Ride the Highest Exterior Elevator in Europe

The Hammetschwand-Lift, which will take you 152.8 meters up the side of a mountain in 50 seconds, cost 500 million francs to build in 1905. That's a huge sum even by today's standards. But the owners of the nearby Bürgenstock Resort (which opened in 1873) spent that much to give their guests the novelty of riding a rickety rocket of an elevator up a mountain. And this author is glad they did.

Today, the elevator continues to thrill both resort guests and non-guests. The world-record-holding lift is also a survivor. Two world wars, a wood-to-steel conversion, and more than a hundred years of Swiss weather, to name a few of its challenges. But over a century later, it still offers the highest vantage point in the Lucerne area, at over 1,130 meters above sea level. It's also, in the name of Swissness, been made more efficient: in 1935, its speed was increased from 1 meter per second to the current speed of about 2.7 meters per second.

The Swiss have ensured that riding the Hammetschwand-Lift up the mountain isn't exactly a wimpy alternative to hiking. You enter the elevator inside a rock pit in a mountain, which, in Swiss style, you reach via a hiking path. The Bürgenstock Felsenweg path is on a ridge overlooking Lake Lucerne. It's a relatively easy and scenic hike from the resort to the lift, but the point is, you still have to hike 30-35 minutes to get there. Only then can you earn your trip up the mountain.

Like most things Swiss, riding the elevator isn't exactly cheap. At about 10 SF for a one-way trip, you may reconsider: is the 50-second excursion worth the price? And if you have a dog, you'll have to pay for him too. So if you're like this author you may choose another hiking adventure and a one-way ride instead. That's okay, because you can still reach the end point of the Bürgenstock Felsenweg hike (you know, the one you hiked to get to the elevator) from up here. However, bear in mind how far you've come up. You might not realize it, since the Swiss all around you will be hiking down the wooded paths and grassy mountain meadows in their flip-flops and ballet flats. But if you're not quite Swiss enough yet, be sure to wear your hiking boots.

For those who want to linger (or forgo the mountain elevator completely), the Bürgenstock Resort is currently getting a face lift and will be reopening in 2017 500 meters above Lake Lucerne, where it's always been. Interestingly enough, the total amount being invested in its remodeling is 500 million SF, the same price the Hammetschwand-Lift cost in 1905. Coincidence?

In any case, the resort will feature private residences, suites, hotels, restaurants, shopping, golf, tennis, curling, a 10,000 square meter Alpine spa, and that all important location near the famous elevator.

For more information:

Hammetschwand Lift
Open May-October

Bürgenstock Resort
6363 Obbürgen
www.buergenstock.ch/en

56. Go on a Free Drinking Tour

Zurich is sometimes called the Water City. In a landlocked country, is this so strange? Maybe not. Zurich is home to both the Limmat River and Lake Zurich—and both are clean enough to swim in. With around 30 lakeside and riverside bathing facilities and almost 20 other open-air swimming areas, no other city in Europe has a higher concentration of bathing facilities per capita.

Year-round, Zurich's water can be enjoyed in another way—from the city's public fountains. Where can you drink from a public fountain in Zurich? The answer is pretty much anywhere. Zurich holds the record for the city with the most drinking fountains. There are 1,224 of them to be exact. You just might not recognize them.

Many of Zurich's fountains are more like works of art than your basic public drinking fountain. In fact, some of them are filled with both spring-quality drinking water and a 500-year-old history. So impressive are Zurich's fountains, that Zurich Tourism offers guided tours of them.

There is also a blog, *Zurich 1200 Fountains*, which attempts to document each and every fountain in the city. The website features a map of the fountains in case your thirst does not lead you to all of them.

In Zurich, tap water is trendy. The number of fountains prove it and so does Zurich's love for sustainability. After all, tap water consumes 1,000 times less energy than purchased bottled water. It can also be 1,000 times cheaper. But drinking tap water in Zurich's restaurants is expensive because the establishments have come up with a way to capitalize on the city's tap water: they call it Züri-Wasser—and they charge you about $4 a glass to drink it. It's still usually cheaper than ordering bottled water, however.

To enjoy the best of Züri-Wasser, take Zurich Tourism's

fountain tour. Our bodies need two to three liters of water every day anyway, as if you needed an excuse to attend. If you can, do your water tour Swiss style, with a Swiss-made Sigg Bottle. These bottles are available in many shops, including larger Swiss grocery stores like Migros (there's even a Sigg bottle on display in the Museum of Modern Art in New York).

Most of Zurich's fountains dispense tap water—in other words, they spew out a mix of 70 percent lake water, 15 percent ground water, and 15 percent spring water. But around 400 of Zurich's fountains are fed with 100 percent spring water. The fun is to find them. One way to find the spring-fed water fountains is to watch the locals: at the fountains with pure spring water, you'll often see locals filling up multiple bottles to transport to their kitchens.

If you need a hint to get started, one of the spring-fed fountains is at the Napfplatz. Also, 80 of the spring water fountains were designed by Alf Aebersold in 1973 as part of an emergency water fountain project, since spring water guarantees a constant supply of water due to its independent source. Find the bronze fountain at Seefeldstrasse and Klausstrasse and you'll start to recognize the others. Many include a drinking section for dogs too. *Prost.*

For more information:

Zurich Fountain Blog:
https://zurich1200fountains.wordpress.com

Zurich Tourism (for fountain tours)
www.zuerich.com

57. Take a Lesson in Humility at a Schoolhouse

The schoolhouse where Heidi author Johanna Spyri was educated is now a museum.

Johanna Louise Spyri, the Swiss author of over fifty novels and children's stories, was born in the rural area of Hirzel in 1827. During summer holidays, she spent time in canton Graubünden, which was later used as a prominent setting for her books.

Spyri wrote her most famous story, *Heidi*, in only four weeks, but it's made a lasting impression on readers since it was first published in 1881. The main character, Heidi, is an orphan girl who was raised by her aunt in Maienfeld. (Maienfeld is much more of a tourist destination than Hirzel—there you can visit an imagined version of Heidi's House—see Idea 30.) At the age of six, Heidi goes to live with her grumpy grandfather in the Swiss Alps. There she befriends Peter, the goatherd neighbor boy, as well as many others, and eventually transforms her grandfather into a happier man. The original story, which was written in two parts, has been adapted more than twenty times for television and film.

The schoolhouse Johanna Spyri attended as a child (built in 1660), is set high above the town of Horgen, and has been converted into a small museum featuring documents, pictures, and books honoring the author's life. It's only open a few hours a week, but never mind that. Visiting Johanna Spyri's birth village—and not the tiny interior of the schoolhouse—is the point of your visit, so go when the desire to do something outdoorsy moves you.

The town of Hirzel feels like a mini Appenzell minus the tourists. There are rolling hills and hiking paths calling your name in every direction. And a silence that screams authenticity—not famous author birthplace.

Hirzel is Switzerland at its most Swiss. A place where fame of global proportions is whispered, not yelled. Fifty million copies of *Heidi* later, nothing in Johanna Spyri's village has changed— which is something to contemplate as you wander up the hill to her birthplace. With nothing except a quiet plaque gracing its exterior, you just might miss Switzerland's most famous author. The cows around the corner though, will be sure to announce their presence.

For more information:

Johanna Spyri Museum
Dorfstrasse 48
8816 Hirzel
www.spyri-museum.ch
By car: Parking lot by the church
By bus: PostBus from Horgen or Wädenswil to Hirzel-Kirche

You can also visit the cemetery in Sihlfeld where Spyri is buried:
Friedhof Sihlfeld
Aemtlerstrasse 151
8003 Zurich

58. Pray to the Black Madonna

You don't have to be religious to enjoy a heavenly visit to Einsiedeln Abbey. Nevertheless, every year, thousands of pilgrims make the journey via the Way of St. James to the thousand-year-old Benedictine monastery, which perches majestically in all its baroque glory above Einsiedeln's old town. It's especially awe-inspiring at Christmas time, when a tree and market adorns Abbey Square.

Founded in 835 by the Benedictine monk Meinrad, Switzerland's most important pilgrimage site wasn't always baroque. Being over a thousand years old, the abbey naturally underwent several stylistic makeovers: It was born Romanesque, later became Gothic, and finally grew into its current baroque design.

History lives at Einsiedeln Abbey. Pilgrims still drink from the Lady Fountain. Monks still gather daily for services in the abbey church. And the monastery school is still in session in the abbey's wings. German services are still offered to the public. And *Salve Regina* has been sung daily at 5 p.m. in the Chapel of Grace since 1817.

Inside the abbey, you'll find stucco and murals. The central dome illustrates a nativity story. The Asam Brothers of Munich created the decorative ceilings in the nave. But the highlight is the 15th century Black Madonna inside the black marbled Mercy Chapel (Gnadenkapelle). Sadly (or perhaps, happily), the Madonna became black over the decades due to dust and soot from candles, oil lamps, and incense. When you think about it, all this dirt is quite an accomplishment, given that most of Switzerland is so clean you can eat your lunch off of a bus floor. In 1803, the hands and face of the Madonna were painted black, perhaps to hide the sad reality that grime exists in Switzerland too.

If you take a daily tour, you'll also gain access to the baroque abbey library, which is not otherwise open to the public. Here, you can study history spanning over 1,000 years via 1,200 manuscripts, 1,110 incunabulum and early prints, and 230,000 printed volumes from the 16th century to today.

Members of Europe's oldest breed of horse, known in Italy as *Cavalli della Madonna*, also call the abbey home. You'll find the horses either grazing in the shadow of the abbey or enjoying their beautiful baroque stable built between 1764 and 1767. Known for their elegance, good character, swinging gait, and robust health, the abbey hopes to preserve their famous horse breed as part of its amazingly long history of success.

Einsiedeln Abbey is also an important gathering point on the Way of St. James. Since the Middle Ages it has served as a meeting place for pilgrims heading towards the Spanish city of Santiago de Compostela. Agnostics enjoy the hiking experience as well. In Switzerland, the easy-to-moderate 460-kilometer Via Jacobi (part of the Way of St. James) leads from Lake Constance to Geneva and features a route strung together by churches, monasteries, and chapels.

Also popular with pilgrims is The Way of the Cross, a 35-minute walk from the southeastern-most point of the abbey's square that follows the Johannis River before rising up to St. Meinrad.

For more information:

Kloster Einsiedeln
8840 Einsiedeln
www.kloster-einsiedeln.ch

Einsiedeln Christmas Market
www.einsiedler-weihnacht.ch

Way of St. James
www.wanderland.ch/en/routes/route-04.html

59. Have Breakfast in a Bath

A hike to the Majingsee is a good excuse for a spa visit.

Good morning, *mitenand*. It's time to put on your swimsuit, sink into the spa, and have a glass of Champagne. It's time for brunch in Leukerbad.

At the Burgerbad, otherwise known as the Leukerbad Therme, your Champagne brunch is served on a floating wooden tray. Swim right up to it and raise a glass to another Swiss wellness experience. Mini sandwiches and orange juice complete the breakfast.

Not a morning person? How about moonlight bathing? However you like your spa experience, Leukerbad and its natural hot springs deliver. Saunas and steam baths. Wellness and fitness. Every day over three million liters of hot spring water flow into the baths here. It isn't the largest spa and wellness resort in the Alps for nothing.

Whether you come for the Champagne breakfast or just

to enjoy the village's thirty thermal baths and its mountain setting below the Gemmi, you'll leave reality behind just as the Romans, Goethe, Guy de Maupassant, and Mark Twain did.

Leukerbad's Burgerbad alone offers ten different bathing options for a surprisingly small price (approximately 23 SF for three hours of bathing pleasure), including a spa surrounded by flaming torches, a heated lap pool that allows year-round outdoor swimming below snow-covered peaks, and an indoor pool with jets that massage various parts of your body in two minute increments. The spa is suitable for all ages—there is a baby spa area, an indoor toddler spa playground, and a 106-meter slide for older children. Do I need to add that it's wonderful?

In Leukerbad, you can become an expert in the healing waters in more ways than one. To appreciate your spa offerings to the fullest, educate yourself as the Swiss do—by hiking. Yes, in Switzerland, knowledge about your surroundings is just a walk away. In this case, take Leukerbad's three-kilometer Thermalquellen-Weg, which begins at the Dorfplatz and leads through the town to the Dalaschlucht. Along this marked path, nine illustrated signs explain the geology, history, and economic impact of the thermal water. The signs are in French or German—yet another educational opportunity for non-Swiss people.

If narrow steel walkways and suspension bridges over rushing water are your idea of fun and adventure, make sure to continue your hike via the Thermalquellen-Steg through the Dalaschlucht, or Dala Gorge. Here a footbridge, which is a meticulous example of Swiss engineering, will lead you four meters above the rushing water through the 600-meter gorge where you can view the source of Leukerbad's mineral waters, where the rocks are streaked with reds, yellows, and greens thanks to their high mineral content. If the weather is cool, you'll see steam rising from the water.

Once you've reached the waterfall, you'll climb a set of stairs that inspires even atheists to pray. Survived? If so, you might as well continue on to the Majingsee. This mountain lake is more like a pond, but the views along the way make it worth the trip. From the Majing Lake, you can take either a paved road back to Leukerbad or descend on a narrow mountain path for a lovely 6.1-kilometer round-trip adventure that's also an excuse to return to the spa to massage your sore muscles.

For more information:

Leukerbad Therme
Rathausstrasse 32
3954 Leukerbad
+41 (0)27 472 20 20
www.leukerbad-therme.ch

60. Photograph 22.6 Kilometers of Ice

View of the Altesch Glacier from Eggishorn.

Exactly 22.6 kilometers of ice. Now that's something to get the camera out for. No matter where your camera takes you around the Aletsch Glacier—the Moosfluh viewpoint, the Bettmerhorn mountain, or the Eggishorn mountain—27 billion tons of ice will be smiling up at you.

A UNESCO World Heritage Site, the Aletsch Glacier is the largest uninterrupted glacier massif in Eurasia. It's so awe-inspiring that you could take the Fiesch cable car (which rotates 360 degrees) up to Eggishorn mountain and spend an entire day standing on the viewing platform. But then you'd be forgoing over 300 kilometers of hiking trails, over 100 kilometers of mountain bike routes, and 35 lift options—many of which let you admire amazing glacier views while enjoying the surrounding scenery as well.

The Eiger. The Mönch. The Jungfrau. Yes, they are there, not that you noticed. Don't worry, even they are used to being upstaged by the Aletsch. There are also the 700-year old stone pines, steppe grassland, and marmots. Don't forget to notice them too.

It's worth spending a week here. Whether you bring your alphorn, a camera, or just a sense of adventure, you'll love the car-free village of Bettmeralp. It's got everything you could want in a Swiss mountain village—easy access to lifts and hiking trails, a Coop grocery store (so groceries will be the same price they are in the rest of Switzerland instead of overinflated as they are at so many independent Swiss grocery stores in mountain towns), and a white church so beautiful that the non-religious might reconsider their status. Bettmeralp also has a lake for paddle boating, scooter rentals (definitely take a ride down to Betten on the scooter), and a sports center with a pool.

One of the best hiking options is the Aletsch Panoramaweg, a 15-kilometer hike that winds around the glacier from Bettmerhorn to Fiescheralp, passing the small but dazzling Lake Märjelen, which has icebergs floating in it. The hike climbs over 400 meters and drops more than 850. Needless to say, there are several steep, rocky sections so hiking poles and an above-average fitness level are recommended. If you want to trek across the ice, you'll need a guide. Trails are typically accessible from June until September.

Which brings us to timing. To see the glacier at its dramatic best, don't come in the winter when the glacier is somewhat indistinguishable from its snowy surroundings. The view from the top of the ski lifts will be disappointing—as will the crowds of snowboarders and skiers who'll look at you with a sneer and say: "Only hiking boots, huh?"

The largest town near Bettmeralp is Brig, which is one train ride (to Betten Talstation) and one cable car ride (to Bettmeralp) away. The trip to Bettmeralp takes 57 minutes from Brig.

For more information:

The Aletsch Arena
www.aletscharena.ch

61. Eat Chocolate and Cinnamon-Roasted Pumpkin Seeds

Every fall in Switzerland there's a pumpkin paradise just waiting to be discovered. It takes place at Jucker Farm, a working farm where towering sculptures made from pumpkins can be enjoyed along with some chocolate and cinnamon-roasted pumpkin seeds and fresh apple cider.

There are two Jucker Farm locations in Northern Switzerland: Seegräben and Jona. Both are wonderful. At lunchtime, each farm restaurant offers a hot buffet with meats and pasta, a salad buffet, soups, sandwiches, *flammkuchen*, and desserts like apple strudel. The food is reasonably priced and very good—which makes finding a table difficult.

Both locations also have a store where fresh produce like apples, pears, strawberries and more can be purchased as well as small gifts. Both locations also have views of the nearby mountains. And both have playgrounds, hay to jump on, seasonal berry or apple picking, and goats to pet. The farms are open year-round.

For a full day excursion in Seegräben, hike from the train station in Pfäffikon ZH along the Pfäffikersee (Lake Pfäffiker) until you reach Jucker Farm. Have lunch at the farm, and then continue your hike along the lake until you return to the train station. The 10-kilometer hike around the lake is easy and can also be done with a stroller.

For a full day excursion in Jona, begin at the train station in Rapperswil. If you have children, you can make a stop at the Knies Kinderzoo, a children's zoo run by the Knie Circus (See Idea 29), on your way to the farm in Jona. From the train station to the farm is about 4.5 kilometers one-way.

It's best if you can manage to visit the farms on a weekday instead of a weekend, as they are quite popular with the locals. Admission is free.

For more information:

Jucker Farm AG
Both locations feature a farm restaurant and playground
www.juckerfarm.ch

Juckerhof
Dorfstrasse 23
8607 Seegräben
+41 (0)44 934 34 84

Bächlihof
Blaubrunnenstrasse 70
8645 Jona
+41 (0)55 212 21 27

62. Gaze at the Madonna del Sasso for a Heavenly View

High above Locarno there are frame-worthy landscapes.

After I visited the Madonna del Sasso, Locarno became my new favorite Swiss city—which was quite an accomplishment, since it rained non-stop for the two days I spent in the "sunniest place in Switzerland."

There is something refreshing about the Italian section of Switzerland. There are palm trees. There are people speaking Italian. And there are buildings painted bright pink, orange, and gold.

One of the gold buildings above Locarno is a famous place of pilgrimage, the Madonna del Sasso, and a visit isn't complete without a walk to it. Devotees like this author take the 20-minute uphill trek from the center of Locarno to the bright sanctuary—even in the gloomy rain. But there's also nothing sacrilegious about arriving at the sacred monument via the funicular (the entrance is near Locarno's main train station).

However you reach Orselina's Madonna del Sasso, you'll enjoy some of Switzerland's most impressive views from its *sasso*, or rock, high above Locarno. From up here, you'll see Locarno and its surrounding villages, Lake Maggiore, and the mountains. And then you'll wonder how it is that the Swiss have remained so down to earth.

If you can pull yourself away from the frame-worthy landscapes, the interior of Madonna del Sasso's neo-Renaissance church is worth a few camera clicks too. Inside the basilica, you'll learn the art of admiration. A statue depicting the Last Supper, Bramantino's 1520 *The Flight into Egypt,* and Antonio Ciseri's *Christ Carried to the Sepulcher* are some of the works of art awaiting your awe.

It might be hard to leave the yellow cliff-side sanctuary (framed in the spring by forsythia), but a waterfall on the pathway back down to reality helps to make the parting a little easier.

As you gaze back up, you might want to say a little thanks to Brother Bartolomeo da Ivrea. In August 1480, he had a vision of the Virgin Mary here. Without his vision, the sanctuary would probably be a modern apartment building instead of an architectural wonder.

For more information:

Sacro Monte Madonna del Sasso
Via Santuario 2
6644 Orselina
+41 (0)91 743 62 65
www.madonnadelsasso.org

63. Drink Beer While Small Children Carry Flaming Turnips

The turnip lantern parade takes place every November in Richterswil.

On the scale of parades featuring flames in Switzerland (see Idea 1), the Richterswil Räbechilbi (Turnip Lantern Parade) is quite tame. But what it lacks in risk it more than makes up for in its ability to celebrate normally ignored root vegetables.

Think 29,000 kilograms of turnips (all grown locally), 50,000 candles, 1,100 participants, and 20,000 visitors (in a town of 13,000) and you'll get the idea. When the Swiss combine the words "turnip" and "festival" they mean business.

The Richterswil Räbechilbi, which has been in existence since the early 1900s, is no small undertaking. In fact, according to the *Guinness Book of World Records*, the Richterswil Räbechilbi is now the largest turnip parade in the world.

In case you're wondering, a *Räbechilbi (Räbenlicht* in High German) is a lantern made from turnips, carved the way

Americans often carve pumpkins. In the Middle Ages, turnips were a kind of modern-day potato—and they were also used in the 19th century as lanterns. Somehow, for reasons that are still unclear, Richterswil residents decided to celebrate their gratitude for the harvest by creating lanterns from turnips and parading them through the town.

Today, the Richterswil Räbechilbi is a tourist event. But it's a very nice tourist event as thousands of twinkling turnips turn the town into a treasure trove in the way only a group of good gourds can. Held every second Saturday in November, the hour-long parade features a procession of individual lanterns made out of turnips and floats created with many lighted turnips arranged in impressive formations such as boats, tigers, whales, and buses.

Houses in the village get a piece of the turnip action too. Residents adorn their abodes with an impressive display of flaming vegetarian goodness. Throughout the town, turnip lanterns are placed on windowsills, doorstops, and even on rooftops. Never mind the fire hazard, it's almost obligatory for houses in Richterswil to be decorated with turnip lanterns, and residents are also asked to turn off their lights during the parade.

Like most Swiss festivals, the Richterswil Räbechilbi also includes a small market (which usually features carved turnips made by children for sale), live music, and a selection of sweets, sausages, and beers. Other towns in Switzerland also celebrate Räbechilbi, but Richterswil's festival is the biggest and most famous.

For more information:

Turnip Lantern Parade
Yearly, Second Saturday in November
Verkehrsverein Richterswil (Event Organizer)
8805 Richterswil
www.vvrs.ch
www.zuerich.com/en

64. Pick Flowers, Fruits, and Berries

There are many places to pick your own fruits and flowers in Switzerland.

Switzerland makes it easy to pick your own berries, flowers, and fruits—there's an entire website that lists participating farms. Pick your season, pick your farm product, then pick, pick, pick.

The rewards for doing a little of your own farming? You'll feel like a local (even more so if you are one), you'll save money (about half the price you'd pay in the store or at the market), and you'll be treated to free smells. Strawberry fields, for example, smell more like a candy factory than a farm.

If you can, bring your own baskets for fruit picking. Some farms may charge a small fee for a cardboard container. If you do bring your own bucket or basket, have it weighed before you begin so that the basket weight can be subtracted from your total fruit weight.

Berry picking can be as organized as a Swiss train schedule, depending on the farm. Often, your picking pleasure may be limited to the row of fruit you are told to pick from. But this is usually to your advantage—if you're given a fresh row, there is no chance of that row being picked over.

Flower picking is usually more free spirited (oh my!) than berry picking and you can often pick when your heart desires, as most flower fields are self-service and open 24/7. Typical flowers for your self-service Swiss bouquet include gladioli, sunflowers, dahlias, roses, and more.

Most Swiss flower fields are typically announced by a handmade sign (*Blumen zum Selberpflücken*). They work on an honor system, and come with and a dull knife hanging on a pole. Bring cash, and unless you plan on picking more than one bouquet, ideally coins. Most flowers are between 60 Rappen and 2 SF. A sharp pair of scissors would make cutting easier and more precise, but is not a necessity.

For more information:

A list of pick-your-own farms in Switzerland
www.selberpfluecken.ch (only in German at press time, but the map is easy to use)

Jucker Farm (see Idea 61)
www.juckerfarm.ch

La Fraisière (Berry farm in Meyrin, only in French)
www.lafraisiere.ch

Ferme Courtois (Farm in canton Geneva—only in French)
www.fermecourtois.ch

Bio Vaud (Farms in canton Vaud that sell directly to consumers—only in French)
www.biovaud.ch

65. Walk Through 26 Cantons

How many countries get to their 700th birthday and think: "I know, let's commemorate it with a hiking trail. Let's represent each member of our population by five millimeters of the trail so we end up with a 34.85-kilometer path. And let's accurately manifest this vision on a precise schedule."

It's fair to say that not many people are as obsessive about hiking (and precision) as the Swiss. But after 700 years, they know who they are. Thus, in May 1991, to celebrate the 700th year since the founding of Switzerland, the Swiss Path was born.

In concept, the path allows you to hike the entire country in 15 hours, as the route recognizes each canton with plaques along the way, naturally organized in the order the cantons joined the Swiss federation. The time you're in each canton coordinates to its population in 1991. Of course.

You can begin hiking the Swiss Path wherever you please, but if you want the proper tour, you should start at the place Switzerland was born—in Rütli. Today, Rütli is only accessible by boat from Lucerne or on foot (a one-hour walk via the Swiss Path from Seelisberg or Treib). It was here, on August 1, 1291, that three men—representing the cantons of Uri, Schwyz, and Unterwalden—shook hands and Switzerland became Switzerland. There's not much here today except a barbecue area, scenic views across the lake, a big rock, a flagpole, and a lot of history. The most historically significant site in the country is quite understated—perfectly representing both the Swiss and their country.

From Rütli, the trail leads around Lake Uri and ends 34.85-kilometers later in Brunnen—where, far from forgotten in the project—the approximately 700,000 Swiss living abroad also have their own dedicated square.

Highlights on the path include:

1. The Schiller Stone, a large boulder rising 30 meters out of Lake Uri and dedicated to playwright Friedrich Schiller, who penned Wilhelm Tell.

2. Tell's Chapel (Tellskapelle) where Tell supposedly leapt to freedom at the foot of the Axen Mountain. It features four frescoes from the Tell legend.

3. Switzerland's largest chime, constructed from thirty-seven bells.

Some sections of the Swiss Path are more challenging than others (some are accessible in winter too), and naturally you can read all about the sections in detail on the weg-der-schweiz website. You can also take shortcuts via boat or train to various sections, as well as choose segments suitable for strollers, wheelchairs, or levels of tolerance for mountainous inclines. Chances are, whatever part you hike, you won't be alone. Estimates show about 200,000 people hike this path every year.

For more information:

The Swiss Path (Weg der Schweiz/Voie Suisse/Via della Svizzera)
Follow the signage, Weg der Schweiz (99)
www.weg-der-schweiz.ch

66. Shop at a Farm Store

Switzerland's greatest food shopping experiences are often in the middle of nowhere.

Some of Switzerland's greatest shopping experiences can be found at a *Hofladen*, or farm store. The most pleasant way to find one is by chance. This author can remember many tiring hikes that were reenergized after finding a farm store selling homemade ice cream, like a treasure on the side of the hiking path.

Swiss farm stores are pleasant for many reasons. Unlike the rest of Switzerland's grocery stores, many are open 24/7. Most are based on wholesome ingredients, including the honor system—and it is a wonderful thing. Simply pick out what you'd like to buy—Organic yogurt? Homemade ice cream? Freshly picked cherries?—and deposit your coins into the shop's cash box. Language skills aren't necessary—nor are math skills. Calculators are often provided, so even adding what you owe is easy and hassle-free.

Shopping at a farm store is a truly Swiss experience, and every *Hofladen* is slightly different—which also makes them fun to discover. Hof Gregori in Bergün sells its organic farm goods inside a huggable red railway car (their homemade ice cream is highly recommended). Family Suter's Hoflädeli in Baden (Baldegg) sells organic products—including tasty apple juice and homemade bread (Saturdays only)—in a tiny room attached to its farmhouse. You simply walk in through the flower-framed door as if you're visiting family. The cows will probably greet you as if you are. In Champfèr, Fadrinas Hoflädeli, a brown chalet, welcomes visitors with yellow shutters and a flower-filled front yard. Inside, it offers Alpine cheeses as well as homemade Engadiner Nusstort (nut pie).

Part of the pleasure is the unexpected shopping—and snacking—when you're in the middle of nowhere. To get started, visit www.vomhof.ch/hof-suche, which allows you to search for farm shops throughout Switzerland, or alternatively, here are a few of this author's favorite Hoflädeli's in various parts of the country:

Zurich Region:

Suter's Oflädeli
Baldeggstrasse 56
5400 Baden-Münzlishausen

(You can take Bus 5 from Baden's Main Train Station to Münzlishausen—the shop is directly across from the bus stop)

Specialties: apples, apple juice, eggs, potatoes, butter, seasonal produce, homemade breads (bread on Saturdays only)

Always open—and while you're at the top of Baden's mountain, you might as well do some hiking too.

Bergün-Filisur:

Hof Gregori (the shop is in a red train car)
Orta 136
7482 Bergün
www.berguen-filisur.ch/sommer/vor-ort/kulinarik/hausgemachtes/hof-gregori.html

Specialties: dried meats, meat for grilling, house sausages, Alpine cheeses, milk, yogurt, ice cream, butter, and much more.

Combine a visit here with the hike from Preda to Bergün (see Idea 94)

Engadine:

Fadrinas Hoflädeli
Via Gunels 1
7512 Champfèr
www.facebook.com/pg/fadrinashofladen/about/?tab=overview

Specialties include: Nut pie, Alpine cheeses, dried meats, organic beer, jam, and eggs.

Other ways to find farm stores (besides by chance):

Vom Hof
www.vomhof.ch/hof-suche (German, French, & Italian)
Here you can search by type of produce, city, and canton.

Schweizer Bauer
www.schweizerbauer.ch (German)

Nachhaltig Leben
www.nachhaltigleben.ch (German)
Here you can search for farm stores and organic shops by zip code

67. Go Hunting and Gathering

Shop at Globus, Jemoli, or Manor and you may be left wondering if any department store is affordable in Zurich. Well, you're in luck. There is one. At more than 110 years old, the Züricher Brockenhaus is an institution as well as a cultural experience. Here, you can find everyday items for un-Swiss prices. The only catch? They're second-hand.

Organized as only the Swiss can be, your shopping experience at this second-hand megastore near Zurich's main train station spans three levels. Be ready for everything from alphorns to *Zwerge* (garden gnomes). Try on designer shoes, find a fondue pot, or pick out a vintage kitchen table. The best thing about this place is its always-changing inventory. The worst part is that it follows the Swiss definition of affordable. This means that a used record can cost 160 SF, a used book about architecture in India can cost 35 SF, and a chandelier can cost 3,500 SF. However, these are good deals in the eye of the Swiss beholder.

There is more to do than shop here. You could spend the afternoon browsing some of the 2,500 books that come in each month while having a drink from the Sirupbar. Author readings, exhibitions, and audio tours also take place here, but you may have to buy tickets in advance.

The store has somewhat limited hours, but to make up for that you can view the most unique items online and place a hold on them for up to 72 hours without being required to purchase them.

For those looking to discard furniture, the store does free pickups—but don't be offended if the Züricher Brockenhaus doesn't want your stuff. The pickup people are picky and your old armoire may not be the right kind of wood. Don't take it personally. A second-hand store that sells over half a million items each year has to have some standards, after all. And the

Züricher Brockenhaus has much, much higher standards than most.

For more information:

Züricher Brockenhaus
Neugasse 11
8031 Zürich
+41 (0)55 555 55 55
Monday-Friday 10 a.m. until 6:30 p.m.
Saturday 10 a.m. until 4 p.m.
www.zuercher-brockenhaus.ch

68. Walk the History of Two Countries along Castle Ramparts

The finest medieval fortifications in Switzerland are so well preserved that they almost look fake, as though Bellinzona's three fortified castles were something crafted for modern tourist amusement rather than medieval defense. The names of the castles impress too: Castelgrande. Castello di Montebello. Castello di Sasso Corbaro. Together, they form a towering example of medieval defensive architecture and appear in the pages of three countries' history books.

Bellinzona has been an important place through the ages—the valley city was at the crossroads of the St. Gotthard, San Bernardino, Nufenen, and Lukmanier passes. The area was once part of Italy, so we have the dukes of Milan, who once ruled northern Italy, to thank for the castle tour—along with the Swiss, who have preserved and renovated these castles as only the Swiss can. This Italian fortification, which was meant to keep the Swiss at bay, became Swiss when the city of Bellinzona joined the Swiss confederation. However, this did not happen until the French occupied Milan and Bellinzona in around 1500. Only then did Bellinzona join the Swiss Confederation to escape the French. *Oui.*

Honor the Italian-turned-French-turned-Swiss castles (now a UNESCO World Heritage Site) by taking a walk (or doing a few cartwheels) on their soft and grassy ramparts. This is a fun activity at any time of day, but especially atmospheric at night when the castle walls are illuminated. Castelgrande, the oldest castle, features an especially nice view of Bellinzona's old town and the surrounding countryside.

While the castles feel purpose built for tourists and are also home to civic and archeological museums, the practically tourist-free town of Bellinzona impresses more subtly. Beyond the three castles are two churches (the Collegiate Church &

Santa Maria delle Grazie) and one beautiful Saturday morning farmer's market on the Piazza Nosetto with local farm cheeses, homemade breads, and salami.

Switzerland's most Italian-looking town is authentic and quiet, and combines Swiss attention to detail with medieval Italian flair. Visit the Teatro Sociale, and you may feel like you're at La Scala in Milan, which was the inspiration for this classical Italian-style theater. Assume the role of a modern Swiss citizen: walk on red cobblestones past the stone gateways and merchants' houses of the old town, get lost in the alleyways, and then find a bench in a quiet courtyard, ready to observe the town like a true local.

For more information:

Bellinzona Tourism
www.bellinzonaturismo.ch

69. Learn Gardening Secrets with the Lazy Gardener

Many people are familiar with the Ricola brand. But if you haven't been in the market for an Echinacea drop or sage tablet recently, then you might not have heard of Alfred Vogel.

Alfred Vogel (1902–1996), a Swiss pioneer of natural health, was known for his organically grown products and his preparation of herbal tinctures using fresh herbs. Convinced that only fresh plants contained the full spectrum of active medicinal substances, he founded Bioforce AG, which distributes herbal tinctures and natural products worldwide.

Vogel, who moved to Teufen in the 1930s, also wrote the 686-page *The Nature Doctor* in 1952, which advised people on the importance of nutrition and lifestyle. (If you're going to listen to someone about the healing powers of nature, all the better if that person made it to the ripe old age of 94.)

While you can no longer hear from Alfred Vogel himself, his protégé, Remo Vetter, carries on the A. Vogel philosophy in Teufen. There, Mr. Vetter organizes tours and tends to the gardens at the Alfred Vogel Museum, located in Vogel's 1930s house.

Mr. Vetter is an organic agriculture expert and author. His book, *The Lazy Gardener*, discusses how to make organic gardening and farming easy—by letting nature do its thing.

True to his book, after my herbal tour, it was time to watch nature at work. So Mr. Vetter and I planted ourselves in his garden with a bottle of Champagne and drank to our good health. Your visit may inspire such lazy gardening tactics too. At the very least, you'll leave determined to buy a white fedora hat, Vetter's signature look.

Inside the A. Vogel Museum you'll find tablet-making machines, homeopathic trituration equipment, glass percolators for manufacturing tinctures, and brown glass jars for storing them. While the museum featuring the production of herbal remedies is limited to a single room, the medicinal herb show gardens, which include around 120 various healing and cooking herbs, are the highlight of any visit.

To complete your Swiss herbal experience, take a hike on the *Kräutererlebnisweg* (30-60 minutes, 2.5 kilometers). Along the route you'll learn about nutrition, stress, digestion, and more. Speaking of digestion, the route ends at the Waldegg Restaurant, where you'll find panoramic views and homemade meals—cooked with herbs from its own garden, naturally.

For more information:

Remo Vetter
9053 Teufen AR
+41 (0)71 335 66 11
The herb garden can be visited year-round, but May through September visits are recommended.
Guided tours in German or English
www.avogel.ch

70. Transport Yourself through Transportation History

Over 20,000 square meters of transport fun.

There is no better place for a transport museum than in a country that has mastered all forms of public transportation. So it's no surprise that if the question becomes "How should I get there?" the Swiss Museum of Transport offers more than one alternative.

Bus. Boat. Train. Car. Choose your favorite method of transport and take it to the museum. The Transport Museum has its own bus stop, boat dock, train stop, and parking lot. And if you prefer to arrive on foot, the museum is a 30-minute walk from Lucerne via an attractive lakeside promenade. Naturally, if you take public transportation, the museum offers reduced admission and transport costs via RailAway (see below).

After celebrating modern transport (in other words, getting there) you can transport yourself into the worlds of steam engines and outer space, or even watch a movie on the largest screen in Switzerland.

The Swiss Museum of Transport organizes its 20,000 square meters of gallery space by mode of transport: trains and trams are in one building, cars are in another, boats in another, and planes in yet another. It even has a building for cable cars (this is Switzerland, people). Scooters you ride yourself connect all the buildings. The museum is also home to a planetarium and a restaurant.

Once you're there, the options are endless. You can drive a train in a simulator, climb onto a historic tram or cable car, fly a helicopter, or walk through a Swissair plane. If you do explore the planes, be sure to take a seat in first class (hopefully this won't be your first and last time) and slide down an emergency exit (hopefully this *will* be your first and last time).

You can also visit the car theater for a show featuring car designs throughout history. Depending how quick you are with the audience buzzer, your language of choice will win out for narration. After the show, you can take pictures of the 344 road signs that decorate the façade of the Road Transport Hall.

Small children love riding the miniature train around the courtyard (annoying extra ticket purchase required), and older ones enjoy watching boats sailing across the new central courtyard. Finally, why not watch the modern boats in action on a lakeside walk back to Lucerne? On your way, you can enjoy an ice cream cone from Confiserie Bachmann, one of this author's favorite places for a treat.

For more information:

Swiss Museum of Transport
Lidostrasse 5
6006 Lucerne
www.verkehrshaus.ch
www.railaway.ch

71. Leave Lake Lucerne to the Tourists (and Go to Lake Lungern)

The lake water here is so clean it's drinkable.

Drink the water or swim in it? At Lake Lungern, you can do both. The turquoise lake is filled with drinking-quality water and one section has a swimming area complete with a sandy beach, paddleboats, and a 56-meter water slide. If the water is too cold to swim in (in the summer, it ranges from about 18 to 24 Celsius), you can also hike or bike around the entire lake (you can rent bikes at the train station in Lungern). Fishing is popular too.

The trail around the lake is flat and easy enough to do with a small baby in a stroller (this author's experience is proof of that) and as a bonus there are no less than seven fire pits along this route—so be sure to bring some sausages as to not have regrets later when you smell other people's picnics. See Idea 38 for more on the Swiss tradition of hiking and grilling.

A worthwhile detour from your lakeside stroll is the nearby two-story waterfall, the *Dundelsbach*. It's located at the southern end of the lake, about 200 meters from Lungern's cable car station.

The small resort of Lungern is about halfway between the popular tourist areas of Lucerne and Interlaken, but is less crowded—and therefore more relaxing—than either of them: five million day trippers visited Lucerne in 2013 alone—yikes! Unlike Lucerne, Lungern has no covered bridge, but its Alpine setting is just as beautiful as either of the more popular resorts. If you need proof of this, watch how many tourists on the Lucerne-Interlaken Express take pictures of this area from the train window. Instead of being one of them, you'll be disembarking from the tourist train for properly focused pictures of greener pastures (that include meadows and forests too.)

Another reason to get off the train in Lungern is to see the one hundred varieties of butterflies that live in the mountain meadows above the town. On the butterfly trail, you'll be almost guaranteed to see butterflies from June through September, not to mention around seventy kinds of wildflowers including pink orchids, yellow milkwort, and violet lilies.

The only downside to the butterfly trail (Schmetterlingspfad Lungern, Trail 575) is that it's quite steep and therefore not for beginners. The usual approach is to take the cable car from Lungern to Schönbüel, then start the hike at the upper cable car station at almost 1,800 meters above sea level, and work your way down to Lake Lungern from there. If you enjoy pain and want to increase your Swissness quotient, you can also begin the trail at the lake and climb up the mountain instead.

For more information:

Lungern Tourism
www.lungern-tourismus.ch

Butterfly Trail (Schmetterlingspfad)
www.wanderland.ch (Trail 575)

72. Play Politics at the Parliament

Most Swiss laws are made here.

Experience direct democracy in the most direct way possible—with a visit to the Parliament Building in Bern. It's here that you can witness the inner workings of the world's most direct democracy—a government that works with its people, instead of for them.

The 1902 Curia Confederationis Helveticae building stands for all that Swiss democracy is capable of—to fully represent the Swiss people, even the sandstone used to create it was imported from different Swiss cities. The architect, Hans W. Auer, was born in St. Gallen and studied in Zurich, thereby democratically representing more than one canton. Thirty-three Swiss artists from around the country were also commissioned to contribute to the building.

Democracy dominates the domed hall, which is the Federal State's national hall of honor. Here, the coats of arms of the original twenty-two cantons of Switzerland surround the Swiss cross at the center of the dome. Four armed foot soldiers, representing Switzerland's four languages, stand watch in the Hall of the Dome too.

Look around. It's here, in the Parliament Building, where most laws are made by a representative democracy comprising the executive branch Swiss Federal Council and the Swiss Federal Assembly, a legislative branch that combines the forty-six-seat Council of States and the 200-seat National Council.

In addition, the concept of direct democracy means the Swiss political system allows its citizens to put almost any law decided by their representatives to a general vote if they see the need. It takes 50,000 signatures within a hundred days of the new law to force a referendum. But because elected officials know how closely the Swiss people monitor their work, the laws they pass are extremely thoughtful and fair—so a referendum happens only about 4 percent of the time.

Direct democracy also allows Swiss citizens the right to propose almost any constitutional amendment they wish, as long as they can gather 100,000 signatures within eighteen months. The only stipulation to proposing an amendment is that it must not violate international law or human rights. Most initiatives proposed by minority groups fail at the ballot box, but they all have an equal chance to be put to a vote in Switzerland.

No one loves independence and autonomy more than the Swiss, so each municipality and canton also has its own constitution. Interestingly, the parts of the country where the people are more likely to participate politically have both stronger economies and superior public services.

For more information:

Parliament Building
Bundesplatz 3
3005 Bern
www.parlament.ch (naturally the website is very democratically presented in five languages, including English)

Tours are free and offered in four languages. It's a good idea to register for your tour the day before by calling +41 (0)58 322 90 22. Check the website for schedules.

73. Admire Art and Architecture

The building echoes both the rolling landscape and the trademark lines in Paul Klee's artwork.

Paul Klee once said, "Everywhere all I see is architecture, line rhythms, plane rhythms." The design of the Paul Klee Center on Bern's eastern outskirts couldn't honor its artist more appropriately. Part art museum, part architectural marvel, it's the place to go to appreciate both Switzerland's most famous abstract artist and modern Italy's star architect.

The museum, which was commissioned by the artist's heirs and opened in 2005, owns more than 4,000 works by Paul Klee (1879-1940) and features a rotating collection of them in two exhibition spaces. It also has a wonderful atelier, a music and event hall (Klee was born into a family of musicians and also married one: pianist Lily Stumpf), a creative exploration area for children, and a café.

Designed by Italian architect Renzo Piano (who also created the Centre Georges Pompidou in Paris), the steel and glass building echoes both the rolling landscape of the area as well as the trademark lines in Paul Klee's work. Piano called the building a "landscape sculpture."

The Paul Klee Center is a true work of art, both inside and out. Inside, you can stroll down the 150-meter "Museumstrasse," which connects the three "hills." Outside you can follow a gravel path around the entire building and admire how, when seen from the rear, it almost completely blends into the lines of the landscape. Along the loop, there are a couple of pleasant detours including both a sculpture garden and Klee's grave, which bring the entire experience full circle.

Tips: Take Bus 12 from Bern's Main Train Station to Paul Klee Zentrum. The trip takes about 15 minutes. Alternatively, you could walk from the station through Bern's UNESCO World Heritage old town to the museum, which takes about two hours. The museum has a brochure of recommended walking routes that include other sights along the way, so you may want to consider taking the bus to the museum and then walking back to Bern.

For more information:

Zentrum Paul Klee
Monument im Fruchtland 3
3000 Bern
+41 (0)31 359 01 01
www.zpk.org
Closed on Mondays

74. Mingle with Movie Stars

The *New York Times* once called Art Basel the "Olympics of the art world." It lives up to the hype.

Imagine yourself and 90,000 other guests mingling with artists, gallery owners, museum directors, private collectors, and A-list celebrities competing to admire art supplied by 300 galleries from thirty-something countries. Art Basel is one of the most prestigious art shows in the world, selling works of art with a combined value of between three to four billion dollars, and glimpses of celebrities contemplating their purchase are priceless. Trying to make your way to the front of the crowd for a good look at the featured masterpieces is a sporting event in itself.

Art aficionados be warned: Art Basel is as much a place to be seen as a place to see art. The Swiss art directors I attended Art Basel with were definitely more concerned with spotting Brad Pitt than locating a specific work of art.

But this is an art show, so let's get back to the art. Out of the nearly 1,000 art galleries that apply to be in the show every year, only about 30 percent, or 300 of them, are selected to exhibit work. And just because a gallery is able to participate one year does not mean they will be able to return—every year, galleries must submit a new application to be judged by the Art Basel Selection Committee, which is comprised of famous international gallerists.

The diversity of artwork represented at Art Basel is awe-inspiring. Paintings. Sculptures. Installations. Videos. Prints. Photography. Some of the represented art genres you may not have even considered. Art performance, anyone?

If you enjoy discussions about art as much as working your way through a maze of people to view it, then an Art Basel Conversation might be just the thing for you. During most mornings, outsiders can learn from insiders—including artists, curators, and authors—about topics such as the evolution of performance practice, and the artist as a choreographer, as well as talks featuring prominent artists. Book signings and interviews are offered too.

Even if you don't want to shell out about 50 SF for a one-day ticket to Art Basel, you can still enjoy the site-specific sculptures that appear around town, along with performances by both renowned and emerging artists during the month of June. There's also a weeklong film festival featuring films by and about artists.

Art Basel has been around since 1970, when Basel gallerists Trudi Bruckner, Balz Hilt, and Ernst Beyeler got together and decided that showcasing modern and contemporary artwork of global renown would be a good thing to do in Basel every June. In 2002, Miami Beach wanted a bit of art action too, so Art Basel was launched there as well and is now a reason for Miami Beach to hold a big celebrity event every December. The internationally-minded Art Basel also expanded to Hong Kong in 2013.

Do you need to appreciate art to attend Art Basel? It helps. But what you need to be able to tolerate are crowds and commotion. If you like your art quiet, contemplative, and status-seeker free, then you need to go to a permanent museum, not a temporary one.

For more information:

Art Basel
Every June
Messe Basel
Messeplatz 10
4005 Basel
www.artbasel.com

75. Tee Off over the Highway

Vulpera is home to a golf course, a pool, and a spa.

Most people do not include Switzerland and golf in the same sentence. These people have not been to the golf course in Vulpera. The nine-hole course, set between spas, castles, and mountains in southeastern Switzerland near Scuol, is as storybook as golfing gets—at least if you're there between May and October for the golfing season.

One of the course highlights is Hole 7, which allows you to essentially tee off over the highway. Hole 3 is also lovely, offering an unparalleled view across the valley to the church in Ftan.

If narrow, tree-lined fairways on an incline aren't for you, the Vulpera Golf Club also has a driving range that can be used by anyone during the summer. Non-golfers who want to delete the "non" from their name must take a lesson with a golf pro in order to participate in any kind of golfing activity. Seems only fair when you consider the cars and bikers on the nearby highway.

The Golf Restaurant Vulpera, which serves both regional and international cuisine, is an easy Hole 10. Or maybe your Hole 10 is down the mountain at the spa in Scuol (Bogn Engiadina). Or up the mountain for the "Castle Gourmet" menu at the Schlosshotel Restaurant Chastè in Tarasp. You can't go wrong with any of them after a mountainous game of golf—or even after no golf at all.

Vulpera, while tiny, is a town dedicated to tourism. It possibly has more hotels than houses. Besides its golf course, the town also boasts an outdoor pool and spa, and if its mineral waters don't improve your health, the mountain air will. Vulpera is in the middle of nowhere. But in a good way.

If you can't make it to this tiny region cradled between the peaks of the Silvretta range and the Engadine Dolomites, don't worry: Switzerland has more golf to offer. In fact, there are approximately one hundred golf courses in Switzerland. So while Switzerland and golf will probably never go together like Switzerland and skiing, the Swiss landscape provides the setting for a true Alpine golf adventure—not to mention a 19th (or 10th) hole that includes plenty of cheese and chocolate.

For more information:

Vulpera Golf Club
Via Maistras
7252 Vulpera
www.vulperagolf.ch

To find a club:
Swiss Golf Network
www.swissgolfnetwork.ch

76. Eat Cotton Candy While Kids Shoot Guns

Despite storybook characters (ahem, Heidi) that may make Switzerland appear as sweet as its chocolate, there are a lot of guns in Switzerland—and a lot of people who like them.

According to swissinfo.ch, about two million guns are estimated to be in private Swiss hands. The country had a population of 8.3 million in 2016 and this statistic gives it one of the highest gun ownership rates in the world—mostly because of its militia army.

Switzerland is a country where its citizens are encouraged to be sharpshooters. This includes its children. Learning to shoot a rifle at a young age is considered so important that the canton of Zurich gives its countrymen a day off to celebrate its young shooters.

The holiday is called *Knabenschiessen* and it literally translates as "boys shooting." Since 1991, girls can also compete in the holiday shooting festival (they often win). The winners are crowned shooting kings and queens and their photos are posted prominently on the Knabenschiessen website. Knabenschiessen is the largest youth rifle competition in existence—and the public is invited.

This means that every second weekend in September, you'll have the opportunity to watch children shoot rifles—identical to the ones issued by the Swiss army—in a carnival setting. If you're like this author, you'll spend most of your time eating cotton candy, riding the Ferris wheel, and dancing. But in the midst of it all, you'll most likely hear the sound of alphorn music mixing with gunshots and so curiosity will lead you to the gun hall, *Albisgütli*. Put on some noise-cancelling headphones, step inside, and you'll witness the main event in the form of rows of children lying on their stomachs shooting rifles.

The Swiss learn to shoot at an early age and men in the Swiss military are issued a military rifle that they keep inside their house. Those in the military are required to keep up with their shooting skills during compulsory shooting practices in their neighborhood shooting range (yes, most Swiss villages have their own shooting range). In fact, not participating in shooting practice can result in being fined.

For a country known for its peacekeeping and neutrality, Swiss gun culture can come as a surprise to a tourist or expat, who may witness hundreds of Swiss slinging their rifles over their shoulders as casually as if they were purses before they board the train or bus. But the Swiss are interested in self-defense, not offense. Their gun culture stems from the idea that because the country is small, enemies could invade it quite quickly. Therefore, every reservist should be able to successfully fight their way to their regiment's meeting place—making the hills come alive with the sound of gunfire.

For more information:

Zurich Tourism
www.zuerich.com

77. Say "Ready, Set, Moo" at the Cow Races

Some cheese sellers don't even speak High German at the Flumserberg Cow Races—a true Swiss cultural experience that involves no outside influences, not even of the linguistic variety (although High German is an official Swiss language, many German-speaking Swiss consider it a foreign language—a mother tongue of Germans, not Swiss.) The Cow Races also involve alphorns and flag throwers. And—why not—an artisan showing off his carving techniques with a chain saw.

The Flumserberg Cow Races are part of a traditional Swiss day out every mid-October. So take the train to Unterterzen, ride the connecting cable car to Tannenboden Alp, and then sit back, relax, and try to understand the announcer as he introduces each cow and rider in his local Swiss German dialect.

If one of the cows impresses you, you can bet on her up to 30 minutes before the race, which, in reality, is a two-time trot around a track. Some of the "racing" cows wear decorative bells, some wear floral headpieces (which don't do much for their wind resistance), and almost all of them wear a makeshift saddle.

Once you observe the cows, however, you'll find that many of them are more interested in you, the audience, than the race. But hopefully that's not the cow you've chosen to win.

As mentioned earlier, the event includes a cheese market. Located next to the Sennästube Restaurant, you'll find cheesemakers from Tannenboden, Wiese, Lauiboden, Wildenberg, and Fursch selling their goods. (There are lots of free samples too.) Children will also enjoy a bouncy house, petting zoo, and playground.

If you can't make it to Flumserberg for the cow race, the mountainous area is still an attractive place to visit, and easy to reach from Zurich. In fact, from Zurich you can take the train directly from the city to the cable car that takes you up to Tannenboden Alp. Depending on the season, you can hike, climb (in a new CLiiMBER climbing tower 15 meters high), ski, cross-country ski, sled, dog sled, and toboggan.

For more information:

Alpine Cheese Market & Cow Races
Mid-October
10 a.m. until 5 p.m.
Tannenboden Alp
8898 Flumserberg Tannenbodenalp
www.flumserberg.ch

78. Swim in a Postcard

Hasliberg is home to a bathing lake, many stunning hiking trails, and dwarfs.

You know those pictures of people lounging by mountain lakes so stunning they look fake? Welcome to the reality of Make Every Facebook Friend Jealous, Idea 78.

A better idea? Leave the smartphone at home and keep the secret of Badesee Hasliberg to yourself. Hasliberg is a Swiss municipality in the canton of Bern located near Lungern (Idea 71) and Brienz (Idea 5). The 3,000 square meter bathing lake on Hasli Mountain is manmade, and heats to a good swimming temperature in the Alpine sun. It comes complete with a grassy rest area, blue and white striped lounging chairs, and a European-style sandy beach (in other words, gravel you'd prefer not to be barefoot on). Bring some flip flops and a love of leisure. Sidestroke is the ideal stroke to take advantage of your mountain audience. This lake is where high expectations meet high altitudes.

There is no gate, but there is a small entrance fee of around 4 SF for adults and 2 SF for kids that someone may or may not collect. Paying this fee helps ensure that besides mountain panoramas and the great outdoors, there are also changing areas, bathrooms, and a café filled with inviting tables under sunshades on the edge of the lake. It's the ideal combination of nurture and nature.

Speaking of nature, if you want to live it up at an even higher altitude, the cable car station Hasliberg Twing is a short walk away from the bathing lake. Ride up to Käserstatt and you'll find hiking opportunities both big and small—with an emphasis on small. This is because Hasliberg is home of the Muggestutz, an old dwarf brought to life in the storybooks of Susanna Schmid-Germann. Being Swiss, this dwarf has his own hiking trails, naturally.

The Käserstatt-Lischen Dwarf Trail (3 kilometers, 1.5 hours) tells the story of the "House in Bannwald" while leading you across the high Alpine moors to Balisalp. Created especially for children ages 4-10, this trail features small detours at equally small places like gnome homes, a swing bridge, and a mini cable car.

There is also another dwarf trail located on the Reuti-Bidmi-Mägisalp cable car route. This trail, which is 5 kilometers and takes approximately 2 hours between Mägisalp and Bidmi, features the story of Muggestutz the Hasli Dwarf. Along the route there are mazes, swings, and caves, as well as a cheese shop selling—what else—Muggestutz cheese. There are also fire pits along the way so you can have your proper sausage lunch. The Mägisalp area has a stunning, yet huggable section of old chalets. The gnome trails are not stroller friendly.

If you prefer your mountain experiences dwarf-free, you can hike the Gibelweg, a 3-hour, 6.7-kilometer round-trip mountain trail that begins and ends at Käserstatt. A challenging hike, it includes a 450-meter ascent and descent across mountain pastures that scream with color in the summer. (Your aching quads will probably scream right back in perfect harmony.)

Over on the other Hasli peak, you'll find this author's personal favorite trail of the area, the 10-kilometer Horizontweg, which starts at the Alpen Tower and takes you via Lake Engstlen and Lake Tannen to the Engstlenalp, with the possibility of a snowball fight along the way—even in mid-July. This trail offers amazing views of the Bernese Alps along with dazzling reflections from the waters of the Melch and Tannen Lakes. On the Engstlenalp, there's a historic mountain hotel, a cheese factory, and the possibility of another—definitely cooler—swim.

For more information:

> Natur-und Badesee Hasliberg
> 6084 Hasliberg Wasserwendi
> www.haslital.ch

79. Ice Skate to Candlelight and Hearts

A larger-than Olympic-sized outdoor ice rink. Candles. A heart-shaped colored light at center ice. Hot chocolate. And yes, probably bad 90s music. But bring your own soundtrack like this author does, and you've got the makings for a special Friday evening.

Held every Friday throughout the winter months, *Romantik-Eis*, or Romantic Ice, takes place at the Taegi Sport Center's ice rink in Wettingen. It offers some of the best skating that this author has ever experienced. The groomed rink is 40 x 60 meters (Olympic rinks are 30 x 60 meters), which means there's plenty of space no matter how many skaters show up—and if this author's experience is anything to go by, you'll have a lot of room for those double Salchows and Lutz jumps. Located just outside Zurich, Wettingen is far from the crowded winter resorts.

Taegi is also home to a wonderful indoor and outdoor pool. The indoor pool has a huge slide that begins indoors, goes outdoors, and comes back indoors again—practical for year-round use, a gym, a sauna and solarium, a fitness center, a mini golf course, and a restaurant. The prices are some of the most reasonable in Switzerland.

For more information:

Taegi Sports Center
Tägerhardstrasse 122
5430 Wettingen

www.taegi.ch

Romantik-Eis is on Friday nights, roughly mid-October-mid-March, 7 p.m.-9 p.m.
Entry: 5 SF (or you can buy a 12-entry card for 50 SF)

There are 300 free parking places
Bus 7 from Baden train station or Bus 12 from the Wettingen train station stops right in front of the Taegi Sports Center

80. See How a Landslide Became a Landmark

In case you didn't get enough canyon at "Switzerland's Grand Canyon" (Idea 46), you're in luck. There's another canyon in Switzerland. It's the Grand Canyon of the Val-de-Travers district. Called Creux du Van, it resembles an amphitheater-shaped stage. Its architect? Mother Nature.

The proper name for the rounded head of a glacial valley is a *cirque*, a French word derived from the Latin word "circus." However, don't go to Creux du Van and expect lions, tigers, or elephants. Instead, this natural area is home to ibex, chamois, and lynx—and besides, the Latin word "circus" actually means "circle."

Creux du Van is a natural rocky cirque formed by landslides triggered by melting glaciers. The cirque near Noiraigue is so interesting it makes people hike ridiculously difficult trails for the pleasure of viewing and also frequently inspires cries of, "Nice work, Nature!"

Which begs the question: Do you want to do that? Hike ridiculously difficult trails with a heavy camera on your back to capture how wonderful a landslide can be? Admit it. You do. This is Idea 80, so if you weren't traveling like a local at the beginning of this book, you are by now. Might as well go for the Swiss gold, *mitenand*.

So. One of the best and most physically challenging (i.e. Swiss) ways to discover the beauty of a 1,400 meter-wide and 150-meter-deep cirque is to hop on a train to Noiraigue, a short way inland from the northwest banks of Lake Neuchâtel.

Once you arrive in Noiraigue, you'll disembark and begin your hike. After climbing for about an hour you'll be rewarded with the possibility of dining at a farm restaurant (*métairie*). Enjoy it as a proper Swiss would—especially if it's *Z'nuni* time or exactly noon. (You did time your hike to arrive at the restaurant for one of these proper Swiss-approved break times, didn't you?)

Bon. After you refuel, the *Sentier des Quatorze Contours,* a path known for its fourteen hairpin turns, will lead you to our landslide turned landmark—Creux du Van. Sing your superlatives—you've earned them.

Continue along the edge of the cirque, enjoying the view until you descend via the *Sentier du Single* towards *La Ferme Robert.* If the fountain at the foot of the cliff doesn't refresh you, the knowledge that you'll soon be resting your legs on a train will.

For those who like to enjoy their erosional viewing pleasures *sans* effort, the summit area can be reached via car (but not via public transportation—Switzerland really dropped the ball on this one—or maybe the possibility of public transport slid into the cirque).

For more information:

> Hiking Route: Sentier du Creux du Van
> Noiraigue Train Station – Les OEuillons – Le Soliat – Noiraigue Train Station
> Time: Approx. 5 hours
> Distance: 13.5 km
> Altitude change: 770 meters
>
> By Car: (Really? Are we not local enough yet?) Fine. From St. Aubin, Couvet, or Travers to the Restaurant du Soliat. The Creux du Van cirque is 300 meters from the restaurant.
>
> www.neuchateltourisme.ch

81. Watch Swiss Street Artists Work

The pedestrian bridge between Wettingen and Neuenhof is a good place to watch Swiss street artists at work.

Graffiti stands out in Switzerland. The country is otherwise spotless, so how could it not? But graffiti is also valued as an art form in Switzerland, and many local councils set aside areas for legal graffiti.

Legalized graffiti? It doesn't seem that crazy coming from a country that also built sex boxes for legalized prostitution (whether that should also have been an entry for this book is another topic). In fact, these days in Switzerland, graffiti artists are often tolerated more than someone cycling in a pedestrian zone. Make sense? Maybe not. But at least we can be grateful that a little leniency exists somewhere in Switzerland.

Graffiti wasn't always so accepted, however. In the late 1970s through the 1980s, Swiss graffiti artists worked at night to escape detection, but many were caught and sent to jail. Today, however, you can see the sprayers work by day.

What changed? It's hard to say. Since festivals like Street Parade are only held once a year, perhaps Swiss society decided that spraying was the least objectionable way for people to let out some of their angst. And contrary to popular belief that the country is filled with wooden chalets, Switzerland does have many concrete buildings and therefore a lot of canvases that could use some color.

One of the most famous Swiss graffiti artists is Ata Bozaci, a.k.a. TOAST, who currently lives and works in Zurich. He's been spraying since the 1990s, and his art has appeared everywhere from the U.S. to China. He details his creative process in a book called *Black Ink* and even sells his work online.

Other Swiss sprayers, like Gordian Hertli and Claude Pietro, known as Iceroc, work in pairs to create graffiti duets and have done so for over a decade. They use their spraying to better society through teaching and various projects. In 2012, for instance, they helped to rid an underpass in Niederweningen of sexual slurs. Today the area is a constantly evolving work of art instead.

For more information:

Ata Bozaci's website:
www.atabozaci.com

Graffiti by district in Zurich:
www.zueri-graffiti.ch

Legal graffiti walls in Switzerland and around the world:
www.legal-walls.net

A way-too-short guide to where to see legal Swiss graffiti artists at work:

Canton Zurich

Oberer Letten

Freestylepark Allmend

Rote Fabrik

Canton Aargau

Pedestrian bridge between Wettingen and Neuenhof (Take train to Wettingen and walk five minutes in the direction of Neuenhof to get there.)

82. Eat 49 Kilos of Bread

Switzerland is known for its cheese and chocolate. In the 19th century the Swiss dominated the chocolate world thanks to a solid hundred years of chocolate innovation. Today's Swiss citizens enjoy some of the highest purchasing power in the world, so chocolate is a luxury they can easily afford—which is why it's not surprising that the Swiss eat more chocolate per year than any other nationality on earth (9 kilograms per person—that's 209 bars). Are you keeping up? To be truly Swiss, you'll have to eat 210 bars of chocolate this year. There could be worse goals in life.

The Swiss also rule the cheese world thanks to superstars like Emmentaler and Gruyère. In a country where celebrities are products rather than people, cheese takes a good slice of Swiss fame. Combine Emmentaler and Gruyère for a perfect fondue and you'll taste the epitome of a Swiss legend. But there is one very Swiss food that gets overlooked in all of this cheesy glory, despite being eaten right alongside it: Bread.

To be Swiss, you must know your breads. The Swiss love bread. It's meant to be eaten fresh daily. And if you thought the Swiss ate a lot of chocolate, well, it's nothing compared to their bread consumption.

According to Marktbericht Getreide Brotkonsumstatistik, published in April 2010, the Swiss eat an average of 49 kilograms of bread per person, per year. That's about 98 large loaves. Luckily, Switzerland has over 200 different types of bread, so you won't get bored as you try to keep up during your next Swiss challenge.

Don't know the difference between *Tessinerbrot* and *Bündner Birnenbrot*? After your bread tour of Switzerland, you will be completely cultured in carbohydrate creations.

Here are some Swiss breads to request at your next bakery visit:

Zopf
This is the classic sweet Sunday bread. The Sunday thing is serious, so you won't usually find this bread in a bakery or grocery store on a Tuesday. This slightly sweet, braided bread goes nicely with a little butter and jam. Some Swiss daycares also request this kind of bread for birthdays.

Tessinerbrot
This bread, the "bread of Ticino," is a soft white bread that comes from, you guessed it—canton Ticino, although the bread is available across Switzerland, if you can't already tell based on the German name. This author loves Tessinerbrot for making French toast. Others like it because of its shape—it's comprised of four to six small, attached loaves that are easy to break off by hand.

Bündner Birnenbrot
Birne means "pear" so this bread is filled with dried pears and nuts—a tasty accompaniment to a cheese plate or for a lazy hiker who doesn't feel like making a sandwich but wants a filling snack. The inhabitants of canton Graubünden cannot imagine having Christmas or New Year's without this bread. Stored in a cool place, the bread can last up to two weeks, which is practically an eternity for Swiss bread.

83. Sled Down a Mountain in the Summer

If you let snow limit your ability to sled, you're not Swiss enough yet. So for additional training, you should head to one of the closest mountain resorts to Zurich—Flumserberg—and go tobogganing in your t-shirt on a beautifully constructed all-weather dry toboggan run.

The Floomzer toboggan run, which begins at the Chrüz mountain station at 1,600 meters, is 2,000 meters long. During your ride on the rails, you'll take three loops, zoom up to 40 kilometers an hour through two tunnels, and lose count of the curves as you descend 250 meters and cross the finish line at the Kabinenbahn Valley Station.

If you've worked up an appetite after your summer toboggan run, the Kabinenbahn Restaurant is ready to serve you. In fact, they have created a Floomzer pizza in your honor. It comes with mozzarella, Alpine cheese from the local farm, veal, and spinach.

The Floomzer toboggan is an adventure—and not just for children. This author's mother went down the toboggan strictly for research purposes (or so she claimed) and liked the ride so much she went again.

And if zooming down a snow-free mountain makes you shriek for joy—like this author's mother did—show up at 10 a.m. when the toboggan opens. As of this writing, they have an early bird ticket that allows for unlimited rides between 10 a.m. and 12 p.m.

For more information:

Floomzer Toboggan Run
Bergbahnen Flumserberg AG
Tannenboden
8898 Flumserberg
+41 (0)81 720 15 15
www.floomzer.ch

Restaurant Kabinenbahn
Tannenbodenalp
8898 Flumserberg
+41 (0)81 733 19 71
www.kabinenbahn.ch

84. Watch Caroling Being Redefined

Ah, Christmas in Zurich. Where else can you eat melted cheese from paper plates, admire the number of vendors who attempt to make a living selling socks, and add to your collection of mismatched mulled wine mugs?

Christmas in Zurich also wouldn't be the same without the music. One of the best ways to experience the lost art of caroling is to listen to choirs gracing The Singing Christmas Tree, which has been a Zurich Christmas experience at the Werdmühleplatz since 1998. Over 90 musical performances are staged here, and their mission is to keep the Advent singing tradition alive. All choirs appear on festively arranged risers that allow the singers to stand in Christmas tree formation.

To enjoy the singing to its fullest, you'll want to have some Glüwein (mulled wine) with a side of Heissi Marroni (roasted chestnuts). In fact, while at the Werdmühleplatz, you should probably have several cups of the mulled wine, since out of the five main Zurich Christmas locales tested by the *Tages Anzeiger* in 2015, the dark red drink at the Werdmühleplatz was rated best. (The mulled wine at the main train station was rated worst.) Good or bad, about 2,500 liters of mulled wine are drunk per day at each location—meaning day-after headaches are common, but regrets are not.

With Zurich's top mulled wine in hand, you can raise your glass (or paper cup) to The Singing Christmas Tree, a Zurich moment you don't want to miss. Why? Because The Singing Christmas Tree redefines what Christmas means. Here's the thing: some of the choirs gracing The Singing Christmas Tree are not going to sing a traditional German carol. Chances are, some of the choirs at The Singing Christmas Tree are going to sing "Age of Aquarius" and "Fame."

If you are surprised at not hearing *O Tannenbaum* and other German carols, perhaps you are not local enough yet. The Swiss often prefer to speak English instead of High German, and Christmas does not seem to change this preference. American Broadway tunes are as likely to be sung as anything else.

In any case, the Werdmühleplatz market is small and atmospheric—just like Switzerland itself. An old-fashioned carousel invites children to ride on a swan or a pig, the scent of pine mixes with the aroma of roasting sausages, and the trees are filled with glowing stars. For those wishing to escape the cold but maintain the holiday spirit, a fondue tent beckons. Traditional German carols are perhaps not the point. An authentic Swiss experience is.

For more information:

> The Singing Christmas Tree
> Daily concerts during Advent
> Werdmühleplatz
> 8001 Zurich
> www.singingchristmastree.ch

85. Attend a Cow Fight

If you've committed yourself to this book's bovine bucket list so far, you've watched cows get pretty and you've watched cows race. Now, to complete your Swiss training, you need to watch cows fight.

Cow fighting may seem out of place in a peace-loving country like Switzerland, but Eringer (or Hérens) cows, which come from Val d'Hérens, have a fighting spirit and are bred for combat—not that you'd know it by their sweet sounding names. Samantha vs. Fanny, anyone? Cow fighting has been an official tradition in Switzerland for almost a century—and an unofficial one for much longer. If you want to travel like a local, then you need to take the train to the Valais on a Sunday, where the *Combat de Reines* (Battle of the Queens) takes place. Don't forget your stool, blanket, and picnic. Wine, sausages, and fighting cows—which are surprisingly gentle with humans—will be waiting.

If you go to a regional fight, you'll be part of a crowd of about 4,000. If you go to the final in May, prepare for over 12,000 spectators. Aproz is the place to be if you're a farmer from the Valais.

Many farmers keep their cows in shape by taking them on daily walks—actual fighting cannot be taught—it's wired into each cow's DNA. Those cows that prefer not to fight are always excused from the competition and only cows between the ages of 3 and 11 are allowed to enter.

Swiss cow fights don't have much in common with Spanish bullfights. Instead, the combat is Swiss style—the cow's horns are blunted so they are not too sharp and the battles are bloodless. Some "fights" include nothing but two cows eating grass and drooling in the dirt. In fact, the crowd can be more animated than the cows—this is a culture where cows seem to create more emotion than almost anything else. And as fighting always presents some risk, doctors and vets are always present during the duels.

In the best of fights, you'll see the cows stamp their hooves and lock horns. It's Sunflower versus Buttercup. They push and shove. If it's a really exciting fight, Sunflower might trample a post until finally Buttercup is declared the winner—either because Sunflower retreats and leaves the ring, or because the five jurors have had enough and declare Buttercup "queen."

What's at stake for the winning farmer? A cowbell with a handmade leather collar, worth about 600 SF—and priceless bragging rights.

For more information:

Valais Tourism
www.valais.ch

Fédération Suisse d'élevage de la Race d'Hérens
www.raceherens.ch

86. Enjoy a Rare Swiss Smile

The Hayloft is a 16th century Alpine farmhouse.

The Hayloft is not a hotel. It is not a mountain hut. It is something better. It is the friendliest place you'll stay in Switzerland. That's why this beautiful 16th century Alpine farmhouse is worth a mention as a Swiss experience in itself.

Take it from this author, who has reviewed Swiss establishments for large American travel publishers and received many a cold greeting—if she was greeted at all: you will not get a warmer reception in Switzerland than at The Hayloft.

You can always tell when people enjoy what they do. And for Kerry and Peter Rauber, running a B&B isn't work. It's a labor of love. The resident cattle dog, Anchor, and the cat, Snorkel, also appear to enjoy their work.

Peter, who gave my family a ride to The Hayloft from the Kandersteg train station, welcomed us from the very start.

His farmhouse did too. It's the ultimate Swiss cliché—but in a good way. Geraniums hang from every possible place. The house smiles with authenticity (it was restored using period materials). And inside, chocolate begs to be eaten. Aren't Swiss clichés wonderful?

At The Hayloft, the beds are comfortable and the decor is tasteful. There is no traffic or streetlights, so you'll sleep easy. Even better, you officially become part of the Rauber family for your stay. I have never been to a B&B where the owners actually eat their home-cooked breakfasts and dinners with you. Even the other guests became friends. The owners knew how to make everyone—from our 10-month-old baby to the Dutch retirees in the room next to ours—feel at home.

The location of the Altes Bütschels Hus, the original name of the house, is also fantastic—it's a short 10–15 minute walk from the Kandersteg train station, just far enough away from the main part of town to feel like it's just you, The Hayloft, and the mountains. The house sits in full meadowland glory and comes complete with glacier views, a trout stream, and (why not), a waterfall.

There are many excursions to take from The Hayloft, including a tour of the wild and wonderful Gastern Valley, where Peter grew up. (See Idea 22. Or ask Peter.) Other nearby places of beauty include the Blausee, Lake Oeschinen, and Sunnbüel.

Finally, this is Switzerland, home of the financial experts, so let's talk money. At around 50-60 SF per person, per night, The Hayloft is possibly the most reasonable place I have ever stayed in Switzerland. And also one of the best. Funny how what you pay sometimes has nothing to do with what you get.

For more information:

The Hayloft
Altes Bütschels Hus
3718 Kandersteg
www.thehayloft.ch

87. Discover a City Within a City

Once you're in Fribourg, you won't believe you've never found a reason to go there before. The city is magical—and somehow it took this author until 2015 to go there for the first time. Her head hangs in shame as you read this. She should have gone sooner.

But you can avoid this kind of regret. Go to Fribourg. Go now. Go soon. And go often. Part of Fribourg's appeal is that, like a spool of ribbon, its history unravels in front of you as you walk from the main train station to the Sarine River.

First, the paved streets of the railway station quarter turn to cobblestones. The road begins to wind to lead you gently lower and further back in time. You find the 18th century Maison de Ville proudly decked out with geraniums. You find the 16th century St. George Fountain in the Place de l'Hotel de Ville/Rathausplatz. And then you find the St. Nicholas Cathedral, a Gothic masterpiece with some of the most beautiful art nouveau windows in the world. And then you are satisfied. You sink into a pew and listen to tourists whispering praises, and you think, *what a great city*.

Because really, this is enough. Thirteen cathedral bells chime in agreement. But you're in Fribourg, so you must rise. You must keep walking. You must keep unwrapping a city that keeps on giving. Because a city that speaks two languages has twice the beauty you expected—even when someone told you what to expect. Somehow, there's more.

Which brings us to the Zähringen Bridge. Here, time stops. Here, you stop. That's when you look down and realize, there's another city here. Like a series of Russian nesting dolls, Fribourg contains a city within a city.

Here, the Old City introduces itself to you. *My architecture dates from the Gothic period*, it says. The years before the 16th century nod in agreement as you make your way lower, admiring the old stone buildings and the stunning peninsula setting.

Walk across the Pont de Berne, a wooden bridge lined with (what else?) geraniums, and more options beckon. Climb to the Bourguillon Gate for breathtaking city views? Walk along the Sarine? Or find a treat at a *Boulangerie* or *Patisserie*? Whatever you decide, chances are that "go home" is not it.

For more information:

Fribourg/Freiburg Tourism
www.fribourgregion.ch

88. Sled to the City

How many places do you know where you can take a toboggan to the top of a mountain and slide into the country's largest city? Welcome to both the top and bottom of Zurich. It's an amazing ride between the two.

Uetliberg, nicknamed the Top of Zurich, is the starting point for the ultimate in city sledding. The sled run to Triemli is 3.1 kilometers in length and drops 330 meters in altitude. When snow and ice bring sledding enthusiasts to the mountain, there's a guaranteed laryngitis epidemic.

Since this is Switzerland, the sled path is not only groomed meticulously (no misbehaving snowflakes allowed), but it is also monitored daily. Your sledding pleasure is so important, there is even a sledding hotline to give you trail updates.

Is it icy? Is it slushy? Is it perfect? The Swiss leave nothing to chance, not even a trip to the sled hill (well, mountain). Call the toboggan hotline or download a map of the route from the utokulm.ch website. When sledding in Switzerland, you do not just go where the snow and spirit take you. You must sled with purpose.

You can also sled with something else: a flashlight. In fact, zooming down an icy mountain at night with any combination of battery-powered lighting is encouraged. Be your own little shooting star by wearing a headlamp or, better yet, mount your smart phone on your sled and let it be your guiding light as you slide down to the city.

Obviously dark thrills are not for all. There are trees, fences, posts, pylons, and people, and if that combination is a bit worrying for you on an icy incline, don't fret. If sledding isn't your thing, you can still enjoy a scenic 18-minute ride down the mountain on the red S10 train that runs between Triemli and Uetliberg every 30 minutes.

There's more to do up at Uetliberg than sled. You can sit

on a bench and enjoy views of Zurich, the lake, and the Alps. You can hike on countless trails, or you can have hot chocolate at the Uto Kulm Hotel and enjoy the great outdoors from the warmth (and safety) of a restaurant.

For more information:

Schlittelweg: Uetliberg to Triemli, 3.1 km
Sled hotline: +41 (0)44 412 14 71
Starting point: From Zurich, take the S10 to Uetliberg, look for the Schlittelweg sign
Wearing a helmet is recommended
www.uetliberg.ch

Hotel Uto Kulm
8143 Uetliberg Zurich
www.utokulm.ch

Sled Rental
Usually available at Restaurant Gmüetliberg (50 meters from the beginning of the sled run) or at the Uetliberg train station.

89. Admire One of the World's Most Expensive Christmas Trees

Around 140 different vendors sell goods at the Christmas market in Zurich's main train station.

Zurich sparkles—and not just in the snow. Step inside Zurich's main train station during Advent, and you can't help but notice that in Switzerland, even the transport hubs glimmer. During the holiday season, a 15-meter Christmas tree, which takes 362 hours to decorate, glitters with over 7,000 Swarovski crystals in the middle of one of Europe's largest indoor Christmas markets.

If you can pull yourself out of the Christmas market at Switzerland's largest railway station, you'll see that around 12,000 clear and colored Christmas lights, suspended above Zurich's streets like stars, will serve as your guide in discovering Zurich's most beautiful areas. If it all seems too perfect to be real, consider this: diamonds in the sky just kind of come standard in a country with the second highest percentage of millionaires in the world.

In 2012, Zurich was named the world's most expensive city by the Economist Intelligence Unit. If you walk down the *Bahnhofstrasse*, filled with Mont Blancs, Tissots, and Rolexes shining in shop windows, you'll realize something else: This isn't just a country that oozes luxury—it's a country that practically invented it.

Switzerland's most expensive tree—at least as unscientifically estimated by this author—seems right at home in this pricey city, where a pint of ice cream can cost 12 SF and a baby stroller can set you back 1,600 SF. So a million-dollar tree is probably pocket change—at least for the woman who was once in front of yours truly buying her bottle of Coke at the Coop grocery store with a 1,000 SF bill.

'Tis the season to buy more than a soda, however. And you're in luck. Because back at the Christmas market in Zurich's main train station, you'll find around 140 wooden chalets selling everything from handcrafted ornaments to homemade candles. You might as well have dinner here too: raclette, crepes, sausage, gingerbread, and mulled wine (although the train station's version is not rated as highly as other mulled wine in Zurich—see Idea 84) are all on the menu. Dinner at the Christmas market is part of the experience, even if the crystal is reserved for the tree instead of your wineglass.

Swarovski, an Austrian crystal company founded in 1895, is busy at Christmas time—its work isn't just featured on Zurich's tree, but on trees around the world. A 250-kilogram Swarovski crystal star currently tops the Rockefeller Christmas Tree in New York City. There are also Swarovski trees in Paris, Shanghai, Rio de Janeiro, and in the company's home city, Innsbruck. But in this author's admittedly very biased opinion, it's hard to top the sparkle of the Christmas tree in Zurich—not the least because the entire city reflects its elegance.

For more information:

Christkindlimarkt
Zurich Main Railway Station
8001 Zurich
Late November-December 24
www.christkindlimarkt.ch

Swarovski ornaments are available at:
Swarovski Boutique Zurich
Bahnhofplatz 7
8001 Zurich

90. Buy Fabric Fit for a Queen.
Or a Hollywood Movie Star.

Movie stars and royalty wear the fabrics of Jakob Schlaepfer.

What do Coco Chanel, the Queen of England, Nicole Kidman, and Michelle Obama have in common? Two words: Jakob Schlaepfer. Every year, this Swiss textile company creates over 1,200 fabrics, selling them to fashion brands and famous clientele. The fabrics inspire everyone from designers to architects and have been on display everywhere from the Metropolitan Museum of Art to the red carpet at the Oscars.

In the 2014 movie *Muppets Most Wanted*, Miss Piggy married Kermit wearing a gown made from Jakob Schlaepfer sequins. In 2015, Nicole Kidman wore a sequin-embroidered Jakob Schlaepfer design on the cover of American *Vogue*. And in 2016, model Lily Cole appeared at the Oscars wearing a haute couture dress with Jakob Schlaepfer fabric made from recycled plastic bottles. It was fashion meets sustainability on the red carpet, and it was one of Jakob Schlaepfer's discreetly experimental designs.

Originally an embroidery company, Jakob Schlaepfer has innovated along with the times, which means today it uses techniques such as laser cutting and digital printing. More than one hundred years old, this textile titan is located in St. Gallen, a city that's been making a name for itself in textiles since the Middle Ages. St. Gallen is also home to the Textile Museum and Textile Library where you can learn more about the famous fabric fabulousness that is this quiet city in eastern Switzerland.

If you want to buy a piece of history (or just admire how far fabrics have come), the Jakob Schlaepfer shop in St. Gallen or Zurich is worth a visit. Satin, tulle, velvet, and fantasy weaves come by the meter. Or how about an experimental fabric that uses metal, varnish, or paper? It's all on display, along with ready-made accessories like shawls, laser-cut flower necklaces, and inkjet-printed hand-rolled silk cashmere scarves. Check the Jakob Schlaepfer website (listed below)—seasonal sales and special stock sales can often be found.

For more information:

Jakob Schlaepfer Shop St. Gallen
Fürstenlandstrasse 99
9001 St. Gallen

Jakob Schlaepfer Shop Zurich
Obere Zäune 6
8001 Zurich
www.jakob-schlaepfer.ch

St. Gallen Textile Museum
Vadianstrasse 2
9000 St. Gallen
www.textilmuseum.ch

91. Get Lost in Time in a Country Known for Timekeeping

Some places in Switzerland haven't changed for hundreds of years. These are places worth going to. Not surprisingly, Swiss transportation goes almost everywhere in the country, including back in time to the 19th century—in other words, to the Verzasca Valley.

From Locarno or Tenero, take the PostBus to Sonogno. For a true Swiss experience of the V-shaped Verzasca Valley, try the easy 13-kilometer walk from Sonogno to Lavertezzo along the Sentiero Verzasca (Trail 74), which will take about 4 hours. If you prefer a shorter walking tour or have gotten a late start (the last return bus from Lavertezzo is around 7 p.m.), get off the bus in Brione, population 193, and start the hike to Lavertezzo from there.

The hike from Sonogno to Lavertezzo features birch trees, larch forests, and peat meadows. In Brione, be sure to stop in the church to look at the frescoes. You may not see many villagers, as the population in the Verzasca Valley is about ten times lower than it was only half a century ago. But some families still carry on the valley traditions of raising sheep, cows, or goats.

Along the way, you'll find stone houses called *rustici* clustered together as if the little villages were clinging to another era as well as to a mountain. Some *rustici* are available as holiday rentals. For a full Verzasca Valley experience, you could spend a week here relaxing, walking, and eating Alpine cheese, *risotto alla Milanese*, gnocchi *di patate*, and *polenta* in the various valley grottos.

If the 25-kilometer Verzasca Valley were a colored gemstone, it would be green. In fact, "Verzasca" means "green water," and the emerald-colored river that follows the Sentiero Verzasca lives up to its name. The water has shaped the rocks that line its course, and some are strategically molded for a little sunbathing—an essential Verzasca Valley experience.

If you finish the hike in Lavertezzo, you'll be saving the best views—or at least the most picturesque bridge—for last. The *Ponte dei Salti,* a double-arched stone bridge, is the region's centerfold. You can even dive here—there's an underwater cave with a depth of about 10 meters. The most famous swimming spot of the valley is next to the bridge, but you'll probably spend more time on the perfectly polished rocks than in the water—which is almost always bracingly cold.

Speaking of cold, if it's winter and you want to escape the crowds, head to Sonogno for ice skating, a 6.6-kilometer round-trip snowshoe trail, and a 7.5-kilometer cross-country ski trail. But make sure to check snow conditions before you go.

For more information:

Trail 74, Sentiero Verzasca
Sonogno to Lavertezzo (13 km, Approx. 4 hours)
Brione to Lavertezzo (5 km, Approx. 2 hours)
www.wanderland.ch

To rent a *rustico*, visit:
www.verzasca.net

92. Listen to Classical Music in a Classic Mountain Village

Ernen has culture. The village, located at the entrance to the Binn Valley, is part of the Federal Inventory of Swiss Heritage Sites (ISOS), which means it has national importance due to its topographical, spatial, architectural, and historical features. In 1979, Ernen was awarded the Wakker Prize for the preservation of its architectural heritage. The little village boasts timber houses from as early as the 15th century, adorned by gardens so beautiful you'll wish the place were larger.

Unfortunately, this author found that she could walk across the village in approximately five minutes, which is disappointing if you've traveled a long way to get here. So yes, to some the classic Alpine village of Ernen—population about 530—might appear insignificant. Which is why, if you like viewing your tiny Swiss villages in all their significant glory, you should visit Ernen in the summer.

Every summer, big names in classical music and literature descend on the upper Valaisan village, which transforms itself from a quiet Alpine town into a global cultural destination and gets a new name: Musikdorf Ernen (Music Village Ernen).

Ernen's music tradition began in the 1970s, when György Sebök became enthralled by the village while on vacation. The internationally renowned pianist was a distinguished professor at Indiana University's School of Music, and decided to offer three-week master classes in the village, founding Musikdorf Ernen in the process. Pianists came from as far as Portland to learn from Sebök in Ernen, where some practiced their lessons in the bomb shelter of the local priest's house. In the mornings and afternoons, Sebök offered solo piano coaching and master classes, and in the evenings there was chamber music.

Later, in 1987, Sebök added the annual "Festival of the Future," which is a leading chamber music event today. Thanks in part to the success of Musikdorf Ernen, Sebök became an honorary citizen of the village (their third in 800 years).

Despite Sebök's passing in 1999, Musikdorf Ernen continues to be the place where high altitude and high culture meet. Every summer during July and August, the festival features chamber music concerts, piano recitals, baroque music, and an always sold-out literature seminar featuring crime novelist Donna Leon.

During these seminars, Leon reminds writers that "books are meant to be entertaining" and that "it's easier to end a book than begin a book." In an interview with *SF Tagesschau*, she said that together with her students, her group functions like "musicians working together."

Speaking of musicians working together, guests of Musikdorf Ernen have included members of the Schumann Quartet, pianists Beatrice Berrut and Konstantin Scherbakov, as well as members of the Baroque Ensemble directed in part by Ada Pesch, who is the concertmaster of the Zurich Opera Orchestra. Pesch plays the baroque violin during the festival.

An evening with the Baroque Ensemble is especially recommended, since the period instruments are played in an equally historic setting. Some festival concerts take place in the 1578 Tellenhaus, which is listed as a Swiss heritage site of national significance for its frescoes depicting the story of William Tell. Other concerts are held in the richly ornate Pfarrkirche Ernen, built between 1510-1518.

For more information:

Musikdorf Ernen
Kirchweg 5
3995 Ernen
www.musikdorf.ch

93. Go to a National Park in a Country that is a National Park

The only park in the Alps categorized as a strict nature reserve.

It's an experience to go to a national park in a country that's practically a national park anyway. But the contrast between the national park and the rest of Switzerland is something that must be experienced. Why? Well, Switzerland's only national park is protected. Which means no jumping into mountain streams. No random sausage roasting. No biking. No dog walking. And no meandering off the trail to pick up a pinecone.

The aim of the Swiss National Park is to allow unhindered natural development without human interference. The fact that the park is protected—the only park in the Alps categorized by the International Union for the Conservation of Nature as a strict reserve—means that there are actually out-of-place sticks and stones lying around near riverbeds rather than concrete shorelines or benches so red you wonder if the paint is dry. The park highlights Switzerland's natural environment at its most unspoiled, rather than its most pristine. And that, along with eagles, chamois, deer, marmots, ibex, and (if you're luckier than this author) edelweiss, is something to see.

Located in the Western Rhaetian Alps in the southeastern corner of the country, the Swiss National Park has a visitor center in Zernez, which is a good place to stop if you're trying to figure out how to plan your time. There is a road leading through the park that travels over the Fuorn Pass to Italy. Unfortunately, it is unexpectedly well traveled—not only by the PostBus, which stops at six places within the park, but also by motorcyclists from Italy and Austria. So if you are within earshot of the road, the peace and quiet you'd expect from such a protected park is nowhere to be found.

Therefore, if you want to experience the park at its finest, it's key to have a hiking plan that takes you away from the roads. This isn't too hard, since there are 80 kilometers of hiking trails that cover twenty-one routes—including two Alpine hikes—within the park. The trails are of various difficulties and lengths, but none are suitable for strollers or wheelchairs.

One option for an easy two-hour hike is Route 16, the Fuorn Valley. The walk starts near the Hotel Parc Naziunal Il Fuorn, which was once a farming estate and is now the only hotel within the park. Before you start, you might want to eat at the hotel, which serves a tasty cheese plate with local hard and soft cheeses. From Parking Lot 6 or the Il Fuorn bus stop (1794 m), you can take the easy 6-kilometer hike through the Fuorn Valley along the crystal blue Fuorn stream. The trail ends at Buffalora (1968 m), where there is another bus stop and parking lot.

For more information:

Swiss National Park
7530 Zernez
www.nationalpark.ch

94. Ride the Rhaetian Rails. Then Photograph Them.

A 21-kilometer hiking route between Preda and Filisur allows you to enjoy the railway both on the train and off.

Oh, a photo of a blurry bush. Nice, a photo of a tourist's head. Great, a picture of a telephone pole. The results of taking pictures from trains may vary, but few of them are frameable. This doesn't stop the tourists, but maybe that's because they don't know about the *Bahnerlebnisweg Albula*, a new hiking trail built for both train enthusiasts and photographers. Part breathtaking landscape, part engineering masterpiece, the 21-kilometer *Wanderweg* route between Preda and Filisur means you can enjoy the UNESCO Heritage Rhaetian Railway both on the train and off it.

The three-stage Railway Adventure Trail Albula runs parallel to the railway line and is dotted with cows and information panels (in German and English). These informative signs tell the history of the railway, from the people who built it to its effect on the area. The first stage of the trail is a 7-kilometer hike that begins in Preda and ends in Bergün, taking around 2.5 hours. The best place to take photos along this route is at signpost 6, where a stunning bridge, a rushing stream, and a mountain backdrop come together—along with views of a red train that completes the picture twice an hour. Due to some narrow sections, the trail is not stroller friendly.

If you decide to hike, make sure that in addition to your camera, you bring plenty of water, as there are no fountains along the route. Taking something to grill is also recommended since the trail offers some spectacularly located fire pits. For dessert (and as a reward for finishing your hike), grab an ice cream from Hof Gregori in Bergün, which sells its organic farm goods inside a red railway car (see Idea 66).

If Bergün looks familiar, maybe it's because you've watched the first movie version of *Heidi*, which was filmed here in 1952. And you're in luck, because if you want to feel like Heidi or Peter while you're here, all you have to do is visit the Hof Plaschair farm in Bergün, where you can rent a couple of goats to accompany you on your hike.

Bergün is also home to the Albula Railway Museum, which takes train enthusiasts on a journey into the past. Here you can have a seat in a simulator and drive the Crocodile locomotive along the Albula line. Or you can admire old stamps and railway models. And for those tired from hiking, watching the museum's videos is a popular activity.

For more information:

The Rhaetian Railway
www.rhb.ch

Hof Gregori
Orta 136
7482 Bergün

Hof Plaschair
Chant da Farrer 124
7482 Bergün
www.hof-plaschair.ch

Albula Railway Museum
Plazi 2A
7482 Bergün
www.bahnmuseum-albula.ch

Tips:

To add another stunning hike from Preda to your itinerary that has nothing to do with trains and everything to do with a place voted to be the most beautiful in Switzerland, see Idea 95.

Those interested in renting a goat from Hof Plaschair Bergün should note that goats can only be rented by groups of at least ten people. Guided goat hikes are also offered.

95. Visit the Most Beautiful Place in Switzerland

Voted the most beautiful place in Switzerland by Swiss television viewers.

Lai da Palpuogna, a mountain lake in canton Graubünden, is the most beautiful place in Switzerland—at least if you believe a 2007 poll run by the Swiss television channel SF 1. While it's probably impossible to pick the most scenic spot in Switzerland, this author agrees that Lai da Palpuogna (Lake Palpuogna) definitely merits a visit.

Walk 30 minutes on a wildflower-strewn trail from the train station in Preda, and you'll find the turquoise lake on the Albula Pass. Framed by Alpine roses and larch trees, the area surrounding the lake may inspire a game of musical benches. Bring a sausage, bring a camera, or just bring your expectations. You can stroll around the lake in thirty minutes on a 1.6-kilometer path, but it's more fun to move from bench to bench, admiring each of the viewpoints they provide. (Note: The trail is not stroller friendly.)

Multiple fire pits along the lake also encourage lingering. Breathe in the scent of pine (or of grilled meat), and admire the crystal-clear blue-green water—but don't bother to bring your swimsuit since swimming is not allowed. That's probably a good thing, since even on a hot July day the water is mountain lake temperature: way too cold.

For a weekend trip, you could combine a visit to Lai da Palpuogna with a hike from Preda to Bergün (see Idea 94). Preda does have a hotel (located 2.1 kilometers from the Lai da Palpuogna), but there is more overnight accommodation in Bergün, which has multiple hotels, a campsite, holiday apartments, and many more dining options. If you don't have two days to spare, it's also possible to do both hikes (Preda to Lai da Palpuogna + Preda to Bergün) in one day if you don't linger too long—but this author is of the opinion that lingering is part of the fun.

For more information:

Bergün-Filisur Tourism
www.berguen-filisur.ch

Start your hike to Lai da Palpuogna from the train station in Preda. Hiking signs will lead you there.

The best time to visit is in October, when the larch trees turn golden yellow.

96. Shop for Reincarnated Rubber

Spend an hour or so watching the people riding Swiss public transport or the cyclists racing by on the streets on Zurich and you'll notice almost everyone is carrying one brand of bag: Freitag.

But Freitag is not just a brand. In Zurich, it's also a landmark. One that sells exactly what you need to be hip in Switzerland—an indestructible, water-resistant rubber messenger bag.

You can't miss the flagship Freitag store; it's located inside a set of stacked recycled train cars. A climb to the top of the shop will offer you views of Zurich's entire fifth district, which thanks to Freitag and the Im Viadukt shopping center around the corner, gives Switzerland's biggest banking city the hipness it once lacked.

The ingredients of almost every Freitag fashion accessory include truck tarpaulin, a second-hand car seatbelt's webbing, and an old bicycle inner tube. Yes, to the Swiss, ever sustainable and practical, there is nothing more beautiful than reincarnated rubber.

This wasn't always the case, however. Before 1993, there was no Freitag bag. There were only two graphic designers, Markus and Daniel Freitag, who were dreaming of a functional, long-lasting, and water-repellent bag in which to protect their creative work. Since they couldn't find one to buy they created one instead. The first Freitag bags were made in the living room of their apartment, and despite the company's far-reaching success (their bags now have an international market), the brothers still serve as the company's creative directors.

Today, such functional fashion makes a statement in Switzerland—and so does the price. Like everything else on this expensive landlocked island, these bags aren't cheap. The popular messenger bags range from about 125 SF to over 300 SF. If you're on a budget but still want a souvenir, consider a change purse or wallet, which starts at a slightly more reasonable 32 SF.

If you want to keep shopping, visit Im Viadukt, which is just around the corner. Im Viadukt is a cultural and commercial attraction created from the transformation of a 19th century viaduct. It features a collection of independent boutiques and Zurich's only permanent indoor market. At Im Viadukt you can find syrup made from local roses, dried wild boar salami, and imported British cheddar that is well worth eating—even in the land of Gruyère (See Idea 40).

You might also enjoy exploring the Lettenweg, a paved trail that runs above the Im Viadukt shops on a former railroad track. At the Hardbrücke train station, you'll find Züri rollt, where you can rent a bike for free.

Also of interest is the Josefswiese Park, which has sand volleyball, a restaurant, a playground, and a splash pad. The park adds a lot of green space to an otherwise industrial area.

For more information:

Freitag Flagship Store
Geroldstrasse 17
8005 Zurich
www.freitag.ch

Im Viadukt
Corner of Limmatstrasse & Viaduktstrasse
8005 Zurich
www.im-viadukt.ch

Züri rollt
Free Bike Rentals (20 SF deposit required)
www.zuerirollt.ch

97. Do Three Sports along a Lake that Borders Three Countries

The bike trail from Romanshorn to Kreuzlingen takes you through apple orchards along Lake Constance.

If you've ever considered creating your own triathlon, a location along a lake shared by three countries is the place to do it. The bike trail that runs 255 kilometers along Lake Constance, or the Bodensee, is mostly flat and wide, making it easy to combine three sports into one fun day out.

You can start anywhere on the path that you choose, but for an organized adventure, here is this author's recommendation:

She likes to begin her triathlon with a swim at the *Badi* in Romanshorn. Then she bikes to Kreuzlingen and has lunch. Finally, she runs across the border to finish in another country and celebrates her journey with a slice of Black Forest cake overlooking the harbor in Constance (Konstanz).

First stop: See Bad Romanshorn (Swim)

A waterslide that puts you at eye level with the town's church steeple, a lap pool, a children's swim area, and a lake that's clean enough to swim in. Warning: The See Bad Romanshorn may be hard to leave. But the bike path is waiting…

See Bad Romanshorn
Badstrasse 50
8590 Romanshorn
(Open May-September)

Second stop: Kreuzlingen (Bike approx. 23 kilometers)

Now you'll get to experience lovely views from a pleasantly flat bike trail heading northwest along Lake Constance. And you'll also see some of the region's famous apple orchards. If you don't stop for lunch at one of the farms before you get to Kreuzlingen, a great place to eat is the MiniGolf Gourmet Restaurant near the harbor, which has surprisingly good salads. Its "gourmet" credentials are questionable, but it's especially nice if you have kids—there is a playground to keep them busy while you eat.

MiniGolf Restaurant
Seestrasse 49
8280 Kreuzlingen
www.minigolf-kreuzlingen.ch

Third stop: Constance (Run approx. 4.6 kilometers)

How can you tell you've crossed the border into Germany? Check the prices—they're in Euros now. Constance is the largest town on Lake Constance. Make sure to explore its medieval old city as well as the harbor and lakeside area. If it's time for coffee and cake (and when isn't it time for coffee and cake?) enjoy a slice of Black Forest cake and a cappuccino on the patio at Restaurant Patronentasche (Hafenstrasse 2, 78462 Konstanz) while you watch the boats go by.

Fourth stop: Train station in Constance to take you back to your bike.

Constance Railway Station
Bahnhofplatz 45
78462 Konstanz

For more information:

Veloland Schweiz
Bodensee-Radweg (Lake Constance Bike Path)
Section mentioned above: Romanshorn–Kreuzlingen–Constance
(You can also make this a multiple-day trip and circle the entire lake, the trail is broken into four stages totaling 255 kilometers.)
www.veloland.ch

98. Tour Zurich's Sweet Side

Secret sweets are ready to be discovered in Zurich.

Many tourists come to Zurich looking for the inside scoop on chocolate. They go to Lindt in search of a factory tour and come away with only the aromas. Those in the know however, contact Kerrin Rousset, who offers Sweet Tours of Zurich. These intimate tours (groups are kept to eight people maximum) offer a taste of the delicious side of Zurich. Even the locals on the tour were treated to tastes of places they had never been to.

Kerrin, a food writer and blogger turned tour guide, loves dark chocolate. Her voice is rich with enthusiasm and her bag is filled with, yes, cocoa beans. This is a guide who knows her chocolate. The Cordon Bleu-trained pastry chefs on my tour agreed—even they mentioned how much they learned.

Kerrin's sweet tooth guides her (and you) to small, family-run businesses in the heart of Zurich. On one of her 2.5-hour tours, you will visit four or five small shops and bakeries. Treats from truffles to hot chocolate to cakes are included, and so is an education on Zurich's 175-year history of chocolate.

When visiting a chocolate shop or bakery, Kerrin recommends inquiring about their specialties or asking what they offer that other shops don't. By asking such a question at Honold, a family-run chocolatier on Rennweg, for instance, you'd be introduced to both Lotti's Best, a crumbly *nougat feuilleté* with tonka bean and a pinch of *fleur de sel* covered in chocolate, and the Honold Trauben, a chocolate treat that features a Regina grape marinated in cognac.

Fine chocolates offer complex tastes. Bite into a *Jeton Fraise* and you might go into flavor shock as an unexpected blend of rose and pepper infuses the strawberry and white chocolate base.

"If the taste changes from sweet to salty and offers various textures, it's high-end chocolate and worth its equally high-end price," says Kerrin.

For more information:

Sweet Zürich Tours
Kerrin Rousset
www.sweetzurich.ch

99. Ride the Bernina Express to its Highest Point

The Bernina Express runs along Lago Bianco.

Ospizio Bernina, one of the most wonderfully haunting and evocative places in all Switzerland, can be reached via the Bernina Express, exactly 25 minutes from Pontresina.

The Bernina Express, run by the privately owned Rhaetian Railway, is the highest train ride in the Alps, and Ospizio Bernina, at 2,253 meters, is its highest station. Here, you'll find the turquoise *Lago Bianco* (white lake). The color is stunning and so is the silence, and if you didn't know any better you'd think it was fake. But this, if you haven't already discovered after reading the previous 98 ideas in this book, is the reality of Switzerland: it's often too beautiful to be true—yet it is true. And that red bench, which looks freshly painted but is perfectly dry, is just waiting for you to sit down and accept the awesomeness that is Switzerland.

There's not much going on at Ospizio Bernina—the tourists are all in Zermatt—but that's the point. Take a few minutes (after the train departs) to admire the stillness and study the yellow hiking signs. From here, you can hike to another amazing place along the Bernina Express route—Alp Grüm.

The route from Ospizio Bernina to Alp Grüm is a fairly easy (in Swiss terms) trail, so you can even hike it (as this author did) with various handicaps, including a stroller and an American nationality.

The first section of the trail follows Lago Bianco. The flatness here allows for endless admiration of the scene's natural beauty—until another red train cuts through it. Then you'll marvel at how engineering can be beautiful too.

Note that there is one small section of the trail that is particularly rocky and steep. While you're watching your step, be sure to keep a look out for sheep. If you're as lucky as this author was, you'll be rewarded for your hiking efforts by a glimpse of an Alpine shepherd and his fluffy white herd.

When you reach Alp Grüm, you'll have views as far-reaching as the mountains themselves. From here you'll see the Palü Glacier, the Bernina Range, the Bergamasque Alps, and the Poschiavo Valley. If that weren't enough, the Bernina Express will pass by occasionally, doing red pirouettes as it descends into the valley. This is where natural and man-made beauty intersect. But you don't have to stand there drooling. Instead, you might as well have lunch. If you're lucky, it's sunny with a 100 percent chance of *pizzocheri*, the buckwheat noodles that are a local specialty. So sit on Restaurant Alp Grüm's terrace and enjoy both the noodles and the view.

Sadly, it might be hard to come down to earth after this, but the good news is that you've already descended about 250 meters from where you started. From Alp Grüm, the Bernina Express will take you all the way from the cool Alpine glaciers to the warm Mediterranean border town of Tirano, Italy. If palm trees are your consolation prize after a long day out, well, *la vita è dolce*—because don't forget, the Swiss speak Italian too.

For more information:

Visit the Rhaetian Railway site to find out more about its popular Bernina Express route
www.rhb.ch

Trail: Ospizio Bernina to Alp Grüm
Hiking time: Approximately 2 hours
From the station Ospizio Bernina, follow the signs to Alp Grüm. You'll first walk along the lake, then you'll enter a forest. The trail leads to the Alp Grüm train station and the Hotel & Restaurant Alp Grüm.
www.alpgrum.com

Over 8,000 farmers grow rapeseed, which blooms every April-May.

99.1-99.9 ADDITIONAL RESOURCES

INDEX OF IDEAS BY

99.1 TIME OF YEAR

WINTER

Take Back Row Seats at the Fire Parade (1)

Ski on "Flat Land" (3)

See Why Flying is Beautiful (31)

Enjoy Surprisingly Un-Swiss Prices (32)

Snowshoe to Fondue (34)

Walk in the Snowy, Candlelit Woods (51)

Ice Skate to Candlelight and Hearts (79)

Watch Caroling Being Redefined (84)

Sled to the City (88)

Admire One of the World's Most Expensive Christmas Trees (89)

SPRING

Admire Flowers (Other than Edelweiss) (4)

Watch a Snowman Explode (7)

Bike 50 Kilometers for Fun (11)

Cheer on Your Favorite Farm Team (16)

Join the Circus (29)

Walk on a Wine Trail (30)

Playground and Language Hop (33)

Hike on Slippery History (50)

Walk Through 26 Cantons (65)

Attend a Cow Fight (85)

SUMMER

Go to Alphorn Camp (2)

Let Loose for an Organized Reason (8)

Bike 50 Kilometers for Fun (11)

Be Seen at a Picnic (12)

Cheer on Your Favorite Farm Team (16)

Eat Brunch with 1,000 Strangers (18)

Mingle Barefoot (19)

Spoil Yourself with Unspoiled Nature (22)

Drink in a Secret Garden (24)

Consider Monday Night Skate an Olympic Event (25)

Swim Across a Lake (27)

Join the Circus (29)

Walk on a Wine Trail (30)

Enjoy Surprisingly Un-Swiss Prices (32)

Playground and Language Hop (33)

Read *A Bell for Ursli* and Hike the Story (41)

Lounge by Lake Cauma and the Swiss Grand Canyon (46)

Hike on Slippery History (50)

Bike to the Top (and the End) of the World (54)

Ride the Highest Exterior Elevator in Europe (55)

Photograph 22.6 Kilometers of Ice (60)

Pick Flowers, Fruits, and Berries (64)

Walk Through 26 Cantons (65)

Learn Gardening Secrets with the Lazy Gardener (69)

Leave Lake Lucerne to the Tourists (and Go to Lake Lungern) (71)

Mingle with Movie Stars (74)

Tee Off over the Highway (75)

Swim in a Postcard (78)

See How a Landslide Became a Landmark (80)

Sled Down a Mountain in the Summer (83)

Attend a Cow Fight (85)

Get Lost in Time in a Country Known for Timekeeping (91)

Listen to Classical Music in a Classic Mountain Village (92)

Go to a National Park in a Country that is a National Park (93)

Ride the Rhaetian Rails. Then Photograph Them. (94)

Visit the Most Beautiful Place in Switzerland (95)

Do Three Sports along a Lake that Borders Three Countries (97)

Ride the Bernina Express to its Highest Point (99)

FALL

Follow the Cows Home (9)

Bike 50 Kilometers for Fun (11)

Cheer on Your Favorite Farm Team (16)

Discover How Swiss Celebrities are Made (20)

Drink in a Secret Garden (24)

Join the Circus (29)

Walk on a Wine Trail (30)

Playground and Language Hop (33)

Read *A Bell for Ursli* and Hike the Story (41)

Hike on Slippery History (50)

Watch Hot Air Balloons Sway to Yodeling (53)

Ride the Highest Exterior Elevator in Europe (55)

Eat Chocolate and Cinnamon-Roasted Pumpkin Seeds (61)

Drink Beer While Small Children Carry Flaming Turnips (63)

Pick Flowers, Fruits, and Berries (64)

Walk Through 26 Cantons (65)

Leave Lake Lucerne to the Tourists (and Go to Lake Lungern) (71)

Eat Cotton Candy While Kids Shoot Guns (76)

Say "Ready, Set, Moo" at the Cow Races (77)

Attend a Cow Fight (85)

ANYTIME

Sleep Between a Waterfall and a Lake (5)

Experience a Tiny Fishing Village with a Larger-Than-Life Atmosphere (6)

Party in a Tunnel (10)

Eat Vegetarian Food Inspired by Meat (13)

Take a Shower in a Parking Garage (14)

See Why Canton Aargau is Cool (15)

Spectate at a Schwingfest (17)

Find Out Why Swiss Brands are More Famous than Swiss Celebrities (21)

Order Potatoes with a Side of Politics (23)

Study the Grandeur of the Abbey Library (26)

Talk to a Sculpture (28)

Admire a Castle Fit for a Mouthwash King (35)

Hike with No Tourists (36)

Experience Red Carpet Treatment (37)

Grill Sausages at 534 Fire Pits (38)

Don't Bargain at the Flea Market (39)

Eat British Cheese in the Land of Gruyère (40)

Bathe in a Brewery. Or a Church. (42)

Go to Liechtenstein (Because You Can) (43)

See Why the Swiss Riviera Deserves its Name (44)

Drink to Swiss Wine Being Rarely Exported (45)

Discover Why Swiss Cheese has Holes (47)

Relax for Exactly One Minute (48)

Border Shop (49)

Celebrate Static Electricity (52)

Go on a Free Drinking Tour (56)

Take a Lesson in Humility at a Schoolhouse (57)

Pray to the Black Madonna (58)

Have Breakfast in a Bath (59)

Gaze at the Madonna del Sasso for a Heavenly View (62)

Shop at a Farm Store (66)

Go Hunting and Gathering (67)

Walk the History of Two Countries along Castle Ramparts (68)

Transport Yourself through Transportation History (70)

Play Politics at the Parliament (72)

Admire Art and Architecture (73)

Watch Swiss Street Artists Work (81)

Eat 49 Kilograms of Bread (82)

Enjoy a Rare Swiss Smile (86)

Discover a City Within a City (87)

Buy Fabric Fit for a Queen. Or a Hollywood Movie Star. (90)

Shop for Reincarnated Rubber (96)

Tour Zurich's Sweet Side (98)

99.2 TYPE OF ACTIVITY

The Liestal parade is filled with burning wagons.

Refer to the map at the beginning of the book. Or visit www.swisstravelbook.com to download a printable map.

BIKE/SKATE/SWIM/GOLF

Bike 50 Kilometers for Fun (11)

Consider Monday Night Skate an Olympic Event (25)

Swim Across a Lake (27)

Bike to the Top (and the End) of the World (54)

Tee Off over the Highway (75)

Swim in a Postcard (78)

Do Three Sports along a Lake that Borders Three Countries (97)

COWS

Follow the Cows Home (9)

Say "Ready, Set, Moo" at the Cow Races (77)

Attend a Cow Fight (85)

FOOD/DRINK

Be Seen at a Picnic (12)

Eat Vegetarian Food Inspired by Meat (13)

Eat Brunch with 1,000 Strangers (18)

Mingle Barefoot (19)

Order Potatoes with a Side of Politics (23)

Drink in a Secret Garden (24)

Grill Sausages at 534 Fire Pits (38)

Eat British Cheese in the Land of Gruyère (40)

Drink to Swiss Wine Being Rarely Exported (45)

Relax for Exactly One Minute (48)

Go on a Free Drinking Tour (56)

Eat Chocolate and Cinnamon-Roasted Pumpkin Seeds (61)

Pick Flowers, Fruits, and Berries (64)

Eat 49 Kilos of Bread (82)

Tour Zurich's Sweet Side (98)

GARDENS/CASTLES/CHURCHES/MUSEUMS

Admire Flowers (Other than Edelweiss) (4)

See Why Canton Aargau is Cool (15)

Find Out Why Swiss Brands are More Famous than Swiss Celebrities (21)

Study the Grandeur of the Abbey Library (26)

Talk to a Sculpture (28)

Admire a Castle Fit for a Mouthwash King (35)

Discover Why Swiss Cheese has Holes (47)

Celebrate Static Electricity (52)

Take a Lesson in Humility at a Schoolhouse (57)

Pray to the Black Madonna (58)

Gaze at the Madonna del Sasso for a Heavenly View (62)

Walk the History of Two Countries along Castle Ramparts (68)

Learn Gardening Secrets with the Lazy Gardener (69)

Transport Yourself through Transportation History (70)

Play Politics at the Parliament (72)

Admire Art and Architecture (73)

HIKES

Spoil Yourself with Unspoiled Nature (22)

Walk on a Wine Trail (30)

Playground and Language Hop (33)

Hike with No Tourists (36)

Read *A Bell for Ursli* and Hike the Story (41)

See Why the Swiss Riviera Deserves its Name (44)

Lounge by Lake Cauma and the Swiss Grand Canyon (46)

Discover Why Swiss Cheese has Holes (47)

Hike on Slippery History (50)

Walk in the Snowy, Candlelit Woods (51)

Ride the Highest Exterior Elevator in Europe (55)

Photograph 22.6 Kilometers of Ice (60)

Walk Through 26 Cantons (65)

Leave Lake Lucerne to the Tourists (and Go to Lake Lungern) (71)

Get Lost in Time in a Country Known for Timekeeping (91)

Go to a National Park in a Country that is a National Park (93)

Ride the Rhaetian Rails. Then Photograph Them. (94)

Visit the Most Beautiful Place in Switzerland (95)

Ride the Bernina Express to its Highest Point (99)

LODGING

Sleep Between a Waterfall and a Lake (5)

Enjoy a Rare Swiss Smile (86)

MUSIC

Go to Alphorn Camp (2)

Watch Caroling Being Redefined (84)

Listen to Classical Music in a Classic Mountain Village (92)

PARADES/FESTIVALS/PAGEANTS/SHOWS

Take Back Row Seats at the Fire Parade (1)

Watch a Snowman Explode (7)

Let Loose for an Organized Reason (8)

Party in a Tunnel (10)

Discover How Swiss Celebrities are Made (20)

Join the Circus (29)

See Why Flying is Beautiful (31)

Watch Hot Air Balloons Sway to Yodeling (53)

Drink Beer While Small Children Carry Flaming Turnips (63)

Mingle with Movie Stars (74)

Eat Cotton Candy While Kids Shoot Guns (76)

SHOPPING

Enjoy Surprisingly Un-Swiss Prices (32)

Don't Bargain at the Flea Market (39)

Border Shop (49)

Shop at a Farm Store (66)

Go Hunting and Gathering (67)

Admire One of the World's Most Expensive Christmas Trees (89)

Buy Fabric Fit for a Queen. Or a Hollywood Movie Star. (90)

Shop for Reincarnated Rubber (96)

SPAS

Bathe in a Brewery. Or a Church. (42)

Have Breakfast in a Bath (59)

SPECTATOR SPORTS

Cheer on Your Favorite Farm Team (16)

Spectate at a Schwingfest (17)

VILLAGE/CITY/TOWN/COUNTRY

Experience a Tiny Fishing Village with a Larger-Than-Life Atmosphere (6)

Experience Red Carpet Treatment (37)

Go to Liechtenstein (Because You Can) (43)

Discover a City Within a City (87)

WINTER SPORTS

Ski on "Flat Land" (3)

Snowshoe to Fondue (34)

Ice Skate to Candlelight and Hearts (79)

Sled to the City (88)

OTHER AMAZING CULTURAL EXPERIENCES
Take a Shower in a Parking Garage (14)
Watch Swiss Street Artists Work (81)
Sled Down a Mountain in the Summer (83)

99.3 LOCATION WITHIN SWITZERLAND

One of Switzerland's best museums is near Lucerne.

NORTHERN SWITZERLAND

Take Back Row Seats at the Fire Parade (1)

Admire Flowers (Other than Edelweiss) (4)

Watch a Snowman Explode (7)

Let Loose for an Organized Reason (8)

Be Seen at a Picnic (12)

Eat Vegetarian Food Inspired by Meat (13)

See Why Canton Aargau is Cool (15)

Cheer on Your Favorite Farm Team (16)

Mingle Barefoot (19)

Order Potatoes with a Side of Politics (23)

Swim Across a Lake (27)

Talk to a Sculpture (28)

Hike with No Tourists (36)

Eat British Cheese in the Land of Gruyère (40)

Bathe in a Brewery. Or a Church. (42)

Relax for Exactly One Minute (48)

Walk in the Snowy, Candlelit Woods (51)

Celebrate Static Electricity (52)

Go on a Free Drinking Tour (56)

Take a Lesson in Humility at a Schoolhouse (57)

Eat Chocolate and Cinnamon-Roasted Pumpkin Seeds (61)

Drink Beer While Small Children Carry Flaming Turnips (63)

Go Hunting and Gathering (67)

Mingle with Movie Stars (74)

Eat Cotton Candy While Kids Shoot Guns (76)

Ice Skate to Candlelight and Hearts (79)

Watch Caroling Being Redefined (84)

Sled to the City (88)

Admire One of the World's Most Expensive Christmas Trees (89)

Shop for Reincarnated Rubber (96)

Tour Zurich's Sweet Side (98)

CENTRAL SWITZERLAND

Ski on "Flat Land" (3)

Snowshoe to Fondue (34)

Ride the Highest Exterior Elevator in Europe (55)

Pray to the Black Madonna (58)

Walk Through 26 Cantons (65)

Transport Yourself through Transportation History (70)

Leave Lake Lucerne to the Tourists (and Go to Lake Lungern) (71)

EASTERN SWITZERLAND & GRAUBÜNDEN

Ski on "Flat Land" (3)

Follow the Cows Home (9)

Drink in a Secret Garden (24)

Study the Grandeur of the Abbey Library (26)

Walk on a Wine Trail (30)

Snowshoe to Fondue (34)

Admire a Castle Fit for a Mouthwash King (35)

Experience Red Carpet Treatment (37)

Read *A Bell for Ursli* and Hike the Story (41)

Bathe in a Brewery. Or a Church. (42)

Go to Liechtenstein (Because You Can) (43)

Lounge by Lake Cauma and the Swiss Grand Canyon (46)

Hike on Slippery History (50)

Watch Hot Air Balloons Sway to Yodeling (53)

Learn Gardening Secrets with the Lazy Gardener (69)

Tee Off over the Highway (75)

Say "Ready, Set, Moo" at the Cow Races (77)

Sled Down a Mountain in the Summer (83)

Buy Fabric Fit for a Queen. Or a Hollywood Movie Star. (90)

Go to a National Park in a Country that is a National Park (93)

Ride the Rhaetian Rails. Then Photograph Them. (94)

Visit the Most Beautiful Place in Switzerland (95)

Do Three Sports along a Lake that Borders Three Countries (97)

Ride the Bernina Express to its Highest Point (99)

TICINO

Admire Flowers (Other than Edelweiss) (4)

Experience a Tiny Fishing Village with a Larger-Than-Life Atmosphere (6)

Bike to the Top (and the End) of the World (54)

Gaze at the Madonna del Sasso for a Heavenly View (62)

Walk the History of Two Countries along Castle Ramparts (68)

Get Lost in Time in a Country Known for Timekeeping (91)

MITTELLAND/BERNESE OBERLAND/VALAIS

Go to Alphorn Camp (2)

Put on Cross-country Skis and Call the Alps "Flat Land" (3)

Sleep Between a Waterfall and a Lake (5)

Follow the Cows Home (9)

Cheer on Your Favorite Farm Team (16)

Find Out Why Swiss Brands are More Famous than Swiss Celebrities (21)

Spoil Yourself with Unspoiled Nature (22)

Discover Why Swiss Cheese has Holes (47)

Have Breakfast in a Bath (59)

Photograph 22.6 Kilometers of Ice (60)

Play Politics at the Parliament (72)

Admire Art and Architecture (73)

Swim in a Postcard (78)

Attend a Cow Fight (85)

Enjoy a Rare Swiss Smile (86)

Listen to Classical Music in a Classic Mountain Village (92)

WESTERN SWITZERLAND

Admire Flowers (Other than Edelweiss) (4)

Follow the Cows Home (9)

Swim Across a Lake (27)

See Why Flying is Beautiful (31)

Playground and Language Hop (33)

See Why the Swiss Riviera Deserves its Name (44)

See How a Landslide Became a Landmark (80)

Discover a City Within a City (87)

ALMOST ANYWHERE

Party in a Tunnel (10)

Bike 50 Kilometers for Fun (11)

Take a Shower in a Parking Garage (14)

Spectate at a Schwingfest (17)

Eat Brunch with 1,000 Strangers (18)

Discover How Swiss Celebrities are Made (20)

Consider Monday Night Skate an Olympic Event (25)

Join the Circus (29)

Enjoy Surprisingly Un-Swiss Prices (32)

Grill Sausages at 534 Fire Pits (38)

Don't Bargain at the Flea Market (39)

Drink to Swiss Wine Being Rarely Exported (45)

Relax for Exactly One Minute (48)

Border Shop (49)

Pick Flowers, Fruits, and Berries (64)

Shop at a Farm Store (66)

Watch Swiss Street Artists Work (81)

Eat 49 Kilos of Bread (82)

99.4 USING THE SWISS PUBLIC TRANSPORTATION SYSTEM

Play the alphorn and cows listen.

Public transport is the best way to see Switzerland if you want to travel like a local. Covering 27,000 kilometers, it's the densest public transport network in the world, which is an achievement, considering the country's terrain. Linking more than 150 Swiss public transport services, it will get you to the middle of nowhere in time for lunch—and not a second late. Plus, a system that makes you regret your tardiness provides the traveler with both a cultural experience as well as a means of transport.

If you're a visitor to Switzerland, be sure to visit www.swisstravelsystem.com to find out how one **Swiss Travel Pass** can make your travel by road, rail, and waterway completely seamless. Of course, you can always buy individual tickets at stations and stops, but the Swiss Travel Pass is the best value if you'll be doing a lot of traveling—it offers unlimited travel on Swiss Federal Railways, PostBuses, Swiss lake steamers, and the local buses and trams of forty-one cities. And it also gives you access to around 480 museums.

Another option is to buy the **Swiss Half Fare Card,** which entitles you to one month (or one year or more) of half-price travel on Swiss trains, buses, boats, and mountain railways (although certain privately owned cable car companies do not honor it). Current price for the one-month card at this printing was 120 SF.

Whatever you do, make sure you have your ticket before you board any mode of Swiss transport. In most cases, tickets are not available to purchase on board and traveling without a ticket can mean a fine of 90 SF or more.

Use the Swiss Federal Railways website (www.sbb.ch) or mobile app to check schedules and price journeys. The mobile app for smartphones and tablets allows you to purchase your tickets on the go.

99.5 SAVING MONEY IN SWITZERLAND

The alphorn is the Swiss national instrument.

Take Advantage of RailAway Offers

Every month and every season, the Swiss transport system joins up with places like ski resorts, zoos, and hotels to offer discounts to riders using public transport to get to their destination. The catch? You have to buy the tickets at your local Swiss train station before you depart. So if you're buying a RailAway offer to the zoo, you need go to your closest train ticket office before you start your journey and buy the rail, transfer, and zoo ticket together.
www.railaway.ch

Try your luck at SuperSaver Tickets

These are limited and train-specific, but if you're lucky, you might find a great train fare (up to 50 percent off) by searching SuperSaver Tickets online. For example, this author once found a ticket from Zurich to Lugano for only 11 SF using SuperSaver Tickets. You must print the tickets yourself or have them sent directly to your mobile phone with the free app to take advantage of these prices.

www.sbb.ch

Ride a bike for free

An ID and a 20 SF deposit are all you need for a day of two-wheel touring in almost any Swiss city. Check city tourism websites for more information.

Rent an apartment instead of staying at a hotel

If you'll be staying in Switzerland for at least a week in one location, try renting a Swiss holiday apartment instead of staying at a hotel. For example, an apartment in Oberwald for six adults and one baby will cost 1,000 SF for the whole week, and you will save money by being able to cook your own meals. Make fondue for six for 50 SF instead of 200 SF by shopping at the grocery store instead of going out.

Most Swiss tourism websites have links to holiday homes.

Eat at grocery store restaurants

Don't want to cook your own food? Then do the second best thing. Eat at grocery store restaurants. Coop, Migros, and Manor all have buffet restaurants that are open during store hours (so don't think of using them for a late night dinner or Sunday meal). For lunch at Coop, for example, you can enjoy penne with mushroom cream sauce and a small side salad for around 11 SF. (Smaller Coop and Migros stores do not have restaurants.)

Drink from the tap

This author has never understood the high prices for bottled water in Switzerland. So instead of BYOB, BYOS—bring your own (very Swiss) Sigg bottle and fill it up with water from Swiss sinks and fountains when you're out and about.

www.sigg.com

If you own a Swiss Train Pass (GA), turn it in before traveling abroad

Before you go on a long trip, give your GA to your local SBB train station. You can do this up to three days before you leave. They then give you a travel card that is valid for use until you leave the country and upon your return, so you don't need to worry about getting to and from the airport without your GA. When you return to your home station, you simply pick up your GA and receive a voucher for use at any SBB. For example, a 13-day trip away could get you an SBB voucher for 126 SF.

99.6 SPEAKING SWISS

Ten days of organized fun, every ten years in Baden.

French. Italian. German. Romansh. If you want to travel like a local, you need to speak at least two of these languages, and perhaps a few others too.

French (Western Switzerland)

To the uninitiated, western Switzerland is more like a region of France than part of Switzerland. The Swiss French enjoy their wine and have large festivals celebrating the grape harvest. They fill their streets with brasseries and outdoor cafés. Any French-speaking Swiss will make it clear that they are *not* French. But be prepared to speak French. In this region, English is at best a consolation prize, and German? Well, the Swiss French prefer not to admit they have anything to do with such a language.

At a bar in the Romandie (With a soccer game playing on the television)

Bonjour, parlez-vous allemand?
Hello, do you speak German?

Oui, mais vous ne voulez pas?
Yes, but you don't want to?

(The bar explodes with cheers for the German soccer team, which has just scored a goal against France.)

Dans ce cas, pourquoi encouragez-vous l'équipe allemande de football?
Then why are you cheering for the German soccer team?

Parce qu'ils ne sont pas la France? Je ne suis pas sûre de bien comprendre.
Because they aren't France? I'm not sure I understand.

Italian (Southeastern Switzerland)

The southern side of the Alps feels like a different world. In fact, should you find yourself in southeast Switzerland, you might wonder if you have accidentally crossed the border into Italy. There is sunshine. There are palm trees. Every other shop is selling ice cream. And the buildings are all painted yellows, oranges, and pinks. Plus, every restaurant serves only two things: pizza and pasta. Suddenly disoriented, you might find yourself needing directions:

Asking Directions in Italian

Mi scusi, come arrivo al Lago di Como?
Excuse me, where is Lake Como?

Attraversare la frontiera? Veramente pensavo di essere già in Italia.
Across the border in Italy? But I thought I was in Italy.

Oh, sono ancora in Svizzera?
Oh, I'm still in Switzerland?

Adesso capisco perchè non si vede smog.
Ah, that explains the lack of grime.

Ma, e le palme?
But what about these palm trees?

E com'è che la gente parla italiano?
And why are people speaking Italian?

Ah, e così, gli svizzeri parlano anche italiano.
Oh yeah, Swiss people speak Italian too. Figures.

German (Most of Switzerland)

Even though German is the most commonly spoken language in Switzerland, you probably won't recognize it. Because it's not the German you learned in school—and it's not the German the Swiss learn in school either. Swiss German is an unwritten dialect with variants that change approximately every mile. Versions of Swiss German can be so different that even Swiss German speakers don't always understand each other. This suits them fine since they appreciate privacy. But for foreigners who don't, here's how you know you're in a German-speaking area: The street sweeper is on constant duty, the shopkeeper is more concerned with wiping down the counter than serving the next person, and small talk doesn't exist.

Speaking German to a Cashier at the Grocery Store

Grüezi.
Hello.

Ich mache eine Party. Deshalb kaufe ich so viele Chips.
I'm having a party. That's why I'm buying a lot of chips.

Aber aus irgendeinem Grund gibt es in diesem Laden kein Bier.
But for some reason there's no beer in this grocery store.

Oder Cheddar. Das ist doch das Land der Käse, oder?
Or cheddar. Isn't this the land of cheese?

Sagen Sie nichts?
Aren't you going to say something?

Irgendwas?
Anything?

Ja! Ich habe eine Cumulus-Karte! Dank der Nachfrage!
Yes! I have a store loyalty card! Thanks for asking!

Romansh (Mountainous Region of canton Graubünden)

Romansh is spoken by roughly 60,000 people—less than 1 percent of the population — who are scattered in tiny, rural towns throughout canton Graubünden in eastern Switzerland. Romansh doesn't appear on food labels or Swiss job search sites. Yet it is an official language of Switzerland, so it appears on formal Swiss documents. But since more and more young people are leaving canton Graubünden, and the forested, mountainous region is sparsely populated to begin with, it's starting to feel a bit empty.

Speaking Romansh to a Cow

Hallo? Ei cheu enzatgi?
Hello? Anyone?

Nua ein tuts auters?
Where the heck is everyone?

Hallo vacca. Ti eis la suletta, che jeu anfla per tschintschar.
Hello, cow. You're the only one I can find to talk to.

Mi plai tiu sgalin. Astgel jeu far ina fotografia da tei?
I like your bell. Can I take your picture?

Di "cheese" = caschiel!
Say cheese!

Wow. Bien Echo.
Wow. Cool echo.

Gesture

Given the frequency of communication breakdowns in Switzerland (at least for foreigners), it's also common to communicate through good, old-fashioned body language. Here are a few acts or gestures you could try, no matter what part of the country you're in:

Kissing the air around someone's cheeks three times.
Hello.

Setting a huge bag on the bus seat next to you.
Sorry, this seat is saved.

Standing inside the entrance of a restaurant for a really long time.
Hi, I'm an American and I have no idea I'm supposed to seat myself.

However you attempt to communicate, remember, in Switzerland, language confusion is nothing out of the ordinary—23 percent of Swiss residents are foreigners. In the world of linguistics, the Swiss are the champions. The rest of us enjoy the breathtaking landscapes with a side of speechlessness.

99.7 KEEPING THIS BOOK ACCURATE

Everything in this book was as accurate as possible upon publication. But if you notice something that's changed, please contact the author. It would be quite Swiss of you to make sure everything is correct, and this author appreciates your role in keeping the book current. *Merci vielmal* in advance. www.swisstravelbook.com

99.8 USEFUL WEBSITES

Calendar of Traditional Swiss Events

Includes Chienbäse (fire parade), Sechselaeuten (burning snowman), and more
www.lebendige-traditionen.ch

Swiss Travel System

How to get around Switzerland via public transport.
www.swisstravelsystem.com

SBB/CFF/FFS

Timetable and ticket sales for Swiss transport.
www.sbb.ch

Swiss Life: 30 Things I Wish I'd Known

A collection of personal essays in which this author discovers that no matter how hard she wills her geraniums to cascade properly, she will never be a glamorous American expatriate—and she'll never be Swiss.
www.swisslifebook.com

One Big Yodel

A blog about what happens when an American lives in the heart of Europe—and then goes home again.
www.onebigyodel.com

Newly Swissed

An online magazine about Switzerland covering the latest trends in Swiss culture, design, events, oddities, and tourism, as well as tips on how to settle in Switzerland.
www.newlyswissed.com

Swiss Tourism

In case 99.9 ideas for organized fun aren't enough.
www.myswitzerland.com

Writer Abroad

Surviving (and thriving) as an international creative person.
www.writerabroad.com

Swiss Info

Swiss news in 10 languages. (Because four official languages just aren't enough.)
www.swissinfo.ch

Zurich Writers Workshop

Writing instruction and inspiration in Zurich.
www.zurichwritersworkshop.com

Swiss Travel Book

This book's official website. Stop by and say hello in any official language of your choice.
www.swisstravelbook.com

99.9 ABOUT THE AUTHOR

Chantal Panozzo spent almost a decade in the land of cheese, chocolate, and people who can pronounce her name. She has written about Switzerland for *The New York Times, Wall Street Journal, Christian Science Monitor, Salon, Vox, CNN Travel, CNN Business Traveller, Fodor's, Die Zeit*, and many others. Her collection of personal essays, *Swiss Life: 30 Things I Wish I'd Known*, landed her on the cover of the highly esteemed Swiss tabloid *Blick am Abend* as the American who saved Switzerland's honor. She is hoping the sequel, *American Life: 30 Things I Wish I'd Known,* will do the same thing for the U.S. because it could really use someone to save its honor too. In the meantime, she would like to remind everyone that you'll find amazing things to do in canton Aargau, the Chicago suburbs, and everywhere in between. Read more at www.chantalpanozzo.com

INDEX

A

Aarau 68
Aarburg Castle 41, 42
Aare 41, 59
Aargau 40, 44, 55, 213, 265, 269, 274
Abbey Library 69, 265, 269, 276
Aebersold, Alf 150
Aelplerfest 43, 44, 46
Affoltern i.E. 127, 128
Albula Pass 246
Albula Railway Museum 244
Aletsch Glacier 159
Aletsch Panoramaweg 160
Alfred Vogel Museum 182
Alpabfahrt 26, 28
Alp Grüm 258, 259
alphorn 9, 4, 5, 6, 30, 47, 50, 160, 200
Alps 14, 19, 32, 82, 114, 118, 152, 156, 206, 228, 240, 257, 258, 278, 286
Appenzell 27, 152
April 11, 20, 21, 31, 128, 214
Aproz 220
Aqua Spa Resorts 113
Ardez 110
Art Basel 195, 196
Arvenholz 95
Ascona 114
August 1 50, 51, 172
Austria 75, 131, 132, 133, 240

B

Baden 11, 23, 25, 33, 34, 67, 68, 104, 106, 113, 114, 120, 132, 137, 138, 175, 176, 208
Badenfahrt 23, 24, 29
Bad Ragaz 80, 113
Bad Zurzach 113
Bahnerlebnisweg Albula 243
Basel 3, 39, 68, 73, 74, 106, 131, 195, 196
Bellinzona 39, 180, 181
Bergün 175, 176, 243, 244, 246, 247
Bern 39, 44, 54, 57, 59, 68, 103, 105, 190, 191, 193, 194, 205
Bernese Oberland 4
Bernina Express 257, 258, 259, 263, 270, 277
Berry picking 170
Bettmeralp 160
Biel 68, 71, 72, 87
Bignasco 145
bike 11, 29, 31, 32, 87, 96, 116, 117, 145, 146, 159, 186, 249, 251, 252, 283
Bogn Engiadina Scuol 111
Böögg 19, 20, 21, 22
Botta, Mario 73, 114, 145
Bozaci, Ata 212
bread 10, 132, 175, 176, 214, 215
Bregaglia Valley 64
Bregenz 131
Brienz 15, 205
Brig 160
British Cheese Centre of Switzerland 107
Broglio 145
Buchs 116, 132
Bunkers 60
Burgdorf 44, 127, 128
Bürgenstock Resort 147, 148

C

Café Conditorei Schober 129
camellias 11
canton Aargau 40, 41, 42, 62, 96, 294
canton Bern 103
canton Vaud 82, 171
canton Zurich 40
Carigiet, Alois 109
Castasegna 64
castle 11, 12, 40, 41, 94, 95, 115, 180
Cauma Lake 123, 125
Caux 12, 119
central Switzerland 13, 50
Cervelat 20, 96, 102
Champfèr 175, 177
Chateau de Aigle 119
Chateau de Chillon 118, 119
Château de Vullierens 12
Château-d'Oex 81, 82
cheese 9, 13, 19, 29, 30, 50, 54, 61, 90, 91, 107, 110, 121, 127, 128, 131, 132, 199, 202, 206, 214, 215, 216, 218, 235, 241, 288, 289, 294
Cheisacherturm 96, 97
Chiesa di San Giovanni Battista 145
children 2, 22, 41, 50, 72, 76, 82, 87, 88, 89, 109, 110, 138, 143, 152, 157, 162, 167, 185, 193, 200, 205, 216, 219, 251, 296
chocolate 8, 19, 54, 121, 129, 131, 162, 199, 200, 207, 214, 223, 228, 255, 294
Chönz, Selina 109
Christmas 154, 155, 215, 218, 219, 229, 230, 261, 272, 275
Christmas market 230
Chur 68, 123
City Lounge 99
Constance 131, 132, 155, 251, 252, 253
cow 5, 124, 202, 220, 289
Creux du Van 209, 210
cycling 29, 212

D

Dala Gorge 157
Disentis 7, 8
Disney World 94

E

e-bikes 14, 145
Ebnat-Kappel 144
edelweiss 10, 12, 47, 51, 240
Effingen 96, 97
Einsiedeln 8, 38, 154, 155
Einsiedeln Abbey 8
Emmental 127, 128
Emmentaler 107, 108, 127, 128, 214
Engadine Valley 95, 110, 114
English 11, 33, 110, 127, 140, 183, 191, 219, 243, 285, 296
Ernen 237, 238

F

Fadrinas Hoflädeli 175, 177
farms 32, 50, 51, 162, 170, 171, 251
farm store 9, 175
Federal Council 54, 190
Federal Wrestling and Alpine Games Festival 46, 47
Federer, Roger 54, 56
festival 12, 19, 20, 23, 24, 25, 26,

29, 30, 82, 143, 166, 167, 196, 200, 238
Filisur 176, 243, 247
fire pits 90, 91, 103, 110, 186, 206, 243, 246
fishing 17, 43, 44
flag throwing 47
flea market 85, 104, 105
Flims 123, 124, 125
Floomzer toboggan run 216
Flower picking 170
flowers 10, 33, 41, 47, 64, 170
Flumserberg 9, 202, 203, 216, 217
fondue 57, 61, 62, 75, 90, 91, 93, 107, 128, 178, 214, 219, 283
Frauenbadi 52, 53
Frautschi, Fritz 4, 5
Freitag 248, 249
French 11, 12, 34, 48, 51, 61, 87, 120, 157, 171, 177, 180, 209, 215, 285
Fribourg 73, 225, 226
Fricktaler Höhenweg 96
Fuorn Pass 240
Fusio 145

G

Gandria 17, 18
garden 12, 14, 34, 63, 64, 73, 105, 140, 178, 182, 183, 193
Gastern Valley 58, 59, 60, 223
Geneva 39, 68, 105, 106, 118, 121, 131, 155, 171
German 34, 46, 48, 51, 61, 69, 79, 110, 115, 122, 129, 138, 154, 157, 166, 171, 177, 183, 202, 215, 218, 219, 243, 285, 286, 287, 288

Germany 61, 64, 75, 94, 131, 132, 252
Glarus 92
golf 43, 44, 148, 198, 207
Goms Valley 8
Gotthard Base Tunnel 30
graffiti 212, 213
Grandhotel Giessbach 13, 14, 15
Graubünden 71, 79, 80, 123, 152, 215, 246, 288
Grotto Pozzasc 145, 146
Gruyère 9, 107, 127, 214, 249, 265, 268, 275
Gstaad 4, 81, 82
Guarda 109, 110, 111
guns 200

H

Habsburgs 40
Hallwyl Castle 41, 42
Hammetschwand-Lift 147, 148
Hardbrücke 108, 249
Hasliberg 205, 206
Hauser, Jürg 67
Heidi 19, 54, 79, 80, 152, 200, 243
hike 9, 12, 14, 40, 58, 64, 79, 80, 88, 90, 91, 95, 96, 109, 110, 118, 123, 124, 127, 134, 135, 137, 147, 157, 160, 162, 172, 173, 176, 183, 186, 187, 203, 206, 209, 228, 235, 236, 241, 243, 244, 246, 247, 258
hiking 9, 11, 14, 31, 58, 72, 79, 80, 96, 103, 109, 123, 124, 127, 128, 135, 143, 147, 152, 155, 157, 159, 160, 172, 175, 176, 186, 205, 240, 243, 244, 258
Hiltl 36, 37

Hirzel 152, 153
history 1, 5, 17, 30, 41, 46, 72, 94, 113, 149, 155, 157, 172, 180, 185, 225, 233, 243, 255
Hof Gregori 175, 176, 243, 244
holiday 19, 20, 21, 50, 200, 219, 229, 235, 246, 283
Horgen 152, 153
Hornussen 43, 44, 45, 47
hot air balloons 81, 82, 143
hotel 13, 14, 59, 63, 82, 88, 95, 110, 114, 206, 222, 241, 246, 283
Hotel Meisser & Restaurant 110
Hotel Restaurant Morteratsch 134, 135, 136
Hugo, Victor 118
Hürlimann Brewery 113

I

ice rink 207
Im Viadukt 107, 108, 248, 249
inline skating 67
Italian 17, 51, 63, 64, 164, 177, 180, 181, 193, 259, 285, 286, 287
Italy 17, 64, 121, 135, 155, 180, 193, 240, 258, 286, 287

J

Jakob Schlaepfer 233, 234
January 81, 83, 85, 137
Jenins 79, 80
Jona 162, 163
Jones, Michael 107
Jucker Farm 76, 77, 162, 163, 171
July 21, 71, 85, 124, 206, 238, 246
June 12, 30, 33, 160, 187, 196
Junkholz 127, 128

K

Kander River 59
Kandersteg 58, 59, 60, 222, 223, 224
Klee, Paul 193
Knabenschiessen 200
Knie Circus 75, 76, 77, 162
Knies Kinderzoo 76, 162
Kreuzlingen 251, 252, 253

L

Laax 123
Lai da Palpuogna 246, 247
Lake Brienz 13, 14
Lake Geneva 118
Lake Lucerne 50, 91, 147, 148, 186, 263, 264, 270, 276
Lake Lugano 17
Lake Lungern 186, 187, 263, 264, 270, 276
Lake Maggiore 11, 114, 164
Lake Märjelen 160
Lake Neuchâtel 209
Lake Pfäffiker 162
Lake Thun 59
La Neuveville 87, 88
Larible, David 76
La Sarraz 11
Lausanne 39, 46, 118, 132
Lavaux 118, 119
Lavertezzo 235, 236
Lavizzara Valley 145
Lenzburg Castle 41, 42
Leon, Donna 238
Les Diablerets 82
Leukerbad 26, 113, 156, 157, 158
Liechtenstein 115, 116, 117, 265, 272, 276
Liestal 1, 3, 29

Ligerz 72, 88
Limmat River 52, 113, 149
Locarno 11, 39, 114, 145, 146, 164, 235
London 73
Lucerne 9, 68, 106, 127, 147, 172, 184, 185, 187
Lueg 127, 128
Lugano 17, 18, 39, 283
Lungern 186, 187, 188, 205
Lutry 118, 119

M

Madonna del Sasso 164, 165, 266, 269, 277
Maggia Valley 145
Maienfeld 79, 152
Matterhorn Gotthard Railway 8
May 11, 12, 53, 67, 79, 96, 106, 110, 111, 117, 123, 148, 172, 183, 198, 220, 251
Migros 10, 50, 61, 150, 283
Milan 30, 180, 181
Mineralbad & Spa Samedan 112, 114
Miss Switzerland 54, 55, 56
Mogno 145
Monday Night Skate 66, 67, 68, 262, 267, 279
Montreux 12, 119
Morges 12
Morteratsch Glacier 134, 135
Moser, Karl 25, 33
museum 34, 57, 115, 140, 152, 153, 183, 184, 185, 193, 195, 196, 244
Museum Langmatt 33, 34
Museum Tinguely 73, 74
music 24, 26, 33, 34, 52, 143, 167, 193, 200, 207, 218, 237, 238

N

narcissus 12, 119
New York City 23, 73, 85, 230
Niederwald 8
Niederweningen 212
Noiraigue 209, 210
November 106, 167, 168, 231

O

Oberwald 9, 8, 283
Orselina 164, 165
Ospizio Bernina 257, 258, 259

P

Palazzo Salis 63, 65
parade 1, 2, 20, 21, 22, 109, 124, 166, 167, 292
Paris 55, 73, 129, 193, 230
parking 8, 17, 38, 131, 184, 208, 241
Parliament Building 190, 191
Paul Klee Center 193
Peccia 145, 146
Piano, Renzo 193
Piccard, Betrand 81
playgrounds 76, 87, 162
Poschiavo Valley 258
PostBus 12, 63, 123, 153, 235, 240
Pratteln 29
Preda 176, 243, 244, 246, 247
prices 13, 85, 105, 178, 207, 252, 283, 284
public transport 11, 14, 32, 80, 91, 92, 125, 141, 210, 248, 280, 282, 292
purchasing power 85, 131, 214

R

raclette 32, 61, 107, 128, 230
RailAway 141, 184, 282
rapeseed 11
Rapperswil 76, 162
Rauber, Peter 58, 222, 223
Reka checks 125
restaurant 9, 36, 37, 62, 79, 88, 123, 127, 138, 162, 163, 185, 207, 209, 210, 228, 249, 286, 289
Restaurant Alp Grüm 258, 259
Rhaetian Railway 243, 244, 257, 259
Rhine River 73, 116
Richterswil 166, 167, 168
Richterswil Räbechilbi 166, 167
Ricola 56, 182
Rist, Pipilotti 99
Rivella 32
Romandie 11, 61, 286
Romansh 7, 285, 288, 289
Romanshorn 251, 253
Röschti Farm 62
Rösti 61, 62
Röstigraben 61
Rousseau, Jean-Jacques 88
Rousset, Kerrin 255
Rütli 50, 172

S

Samedan 114
Sargans 116
sausages 21, 26, 32, 75, 96, 102, 146, 167, 176, 186, 219, 220
Schanzengraben 53
Schaukäserei 127, 128
Schiller, Friedrich 173
Schinznach Bad 113
Schinznach-Dorf 62
Schmid-Germann, Susanna 205
Schwingen 46, 47, 48
Schwyz 50, 172
Scuol 111, 113, 198
Sebök, György 237
Sechseläuten 19, 20, 21
Seegräben 162, 163
Segantini, Giovanni 64
Selden 59
Sennhütte-Stübli 96, 97
September 28, 31, 53, 67, 160, 183, 187, 200, 251
shopping 20, 21, 52, 64, 85, 120, 131, 148, 175, 178, 248, 249, 283
skiing 7, 9, 19, 38, 82, 199
slowUp 31, 32, 117
snowman 9, 19, 20, 292
snowshoe 90, 91, 92, 236
Soglio 63, 64, 65
Solothurn 44
Sonogno 235, 236
spa 23, 80, 95, 111, 113, 114, 148, 156, 157, 158, 198
Spanischbrötli 23, 25, 33
spas 113, 198
sports 44, 47, 160, 251
spring 10, 11, 19, 62, 96, 109, 113, 149, 150, 156, 165
Spyri, Johanna 152
St. Gallen 39, 68, 69, 70, 99, 100, 143, 190, 233, 234
St. Nicholas Cathedral 225
St. Peter's Island 72, 88
stroller 59, 86, 96, 110, 135, 162, 186, 206, 230, 243, 246, 258
St-Saphorin 118, 119
summer 9, 19, 20, 21, 26, 34, 52, 53, 59, 62, 67, 71, 75, 110, 152, 186, 198, 206, 216, 237, 238

Suter's Hoflädeli 175, 176
Swarovski 229, 230, 231
swimming 14, 17, 71, 72, 149, 157, 186, 205, 236, 246
Swiss Alphorn School 4
Swiss Army 60
Swiss Brand Museum 57
Swiss German 19, 44, 87, 123, 129, 202, 287
Swiss Museum of Transport 184, 185
Swiss National Day 50, 51
Swiss National Park 10, 240, 241
Swiss Path 172, 173
Swiss Riviera 118, 119
Swiss Travel Pass 115, 280

T

Taegi Sports Center 207, 208
Tannenboden 9, 202, 203, 217
Tarasp 94, 95, 198
Technorama 140, 141
Tell, William 12, 54, 173, 238
Termali Salini & Spa Locarno 114
Teufen 182, 183
Textile Museum 233, 234
The Hayloft 58, 222, 223, 224
Ticino 9, 17, 121, 215
Tinguely, Jean 73, 74
toboggan 203, 216, 227
Toggenburg 91, 143, 144
tradition 27, 46, 122, 137, 186, 218, 220, 237
Trun 7, 8
Tunnelfest 29, 30
Twann 87, 88, 89

U

Uetliberg 227, 228
UNESCO 57, 69, 118, 159, 180, 193, 243
Unterwalden 50, 172
Uri 50, 172, 173
Urnäsch 26

V

Vaduz 115, 116
Valais 121, 220, 221
Val-de-Travers 209
Vals 114
Verzasca Valley 235
Vetter, Remo 182
Villars 82
Vogel, Alfred 182
Vulpera 198, 199

W

Weber, Franz 14
Weissenberge 92
Wettingen 11, 76, 207, 208, 213
Wildegg Castle 40, 41
wine 33, 52, 72, 79, 80, 85, 90, 93, 118, 120, 121, 122, 218, 230, 285
Winterthur 39, 68, 140, 141
Wirzweli 91
World War II 60

Y

yodeling 47, 96, 143

Z

Zernez 240, 241
Zug 9, 39, 68
Zugerberg 9
Zumthor, Peter 113

Zurich 5, 8, 11, 13, 19, 20, 21, 23, 24, 30, 37, 39, 40, 52, 53, 61, 67, 68, 69, 70, 71, 72, 76, 85, 105, 106, 107, 108, 113, 129, 130, 131, 132, 143, 149, 150, 153, 176, 178, 190, 200, 201, 202, 207, 212, 213, 216, 218, 219, 227, 228, 229, 230, 231, 233, 234, 238, 248, 249, 254, 255, 266, 268, 275, 283, 293
Züricher Brockenhaus 178, 179

ACKNOWLEDGMENTS

Danke to my husband, Brian. Without his job transfer, there would have been no Swiss adventure. The greatest gift a writer and traveler can be given is the chance to live outside their home country, so I have him to thank for the many wonderful years we spent in Switzerland—and our continuing adventures in the country every year. It's impossible to stay away.

Merci to my Swiss-born daughter, who has finally stopped yelling "nein" at the other children on the American playground and reverted to English as a first language. Just like me, she'll always be a little bit Swiss.

Grazie to my parents, Donald and Susan, for always supporting me in whatever I wanted to do with my life and encouraging me to do it—even when it took me thousands of miles away from them.

Grascha fich to both my mother, Susan, and to my mother-in-law, Felicia, who spent many hours watching my daughter while I wrote this book.

Thank you to these friends, writers, tourism experts, editors, translators, photographers, and authors, who have provided encouragement, contacts, photos, Swiss travel passes, travel ideas, and critiques: Philip Graham, Richard Harvell, Kelly Jarosz, Wojciech Jarosz, Tom Kees, Anne Korkeakivi, Emily Lacika, Brian Opyd, Alan Paul, Jill Prewett, Michaela Ruoss, Jean-Marc Vanot, and Marianne Zweifel.

Say Hello. Or Grüezi.

Chantal writes about American life after Switzerland on her blog, One Big Yodel (www.onebigyodel.com). She would love it if you dropped by to say hello in whatever your official language of choice may be. You can also come by her website www.chantalpanozzo.com or follow her on Twitter (@Writer Abroad), or send her an e-mail: chantal@chantalpanozzo.com

If you want to get an automatic e-mail when Chantal's next book is released, you can sign up for her mailing list at www.swisstravelbook.com. Your e-mail address will never be shared and you can unsubscribe at any time.

Word-of-mouth is crucial for any author to succeed. If you enjoyed this book, please consider leaving a review on your online bookseller website of choice or on www.goodreads.com, even if it's just a line or two. It would make all the difference and is very much appreciated. *Merci vielmal.*

www.ingramcontent.com/pod-product-compliance
Lightning Source LLC
Chambersburg PA
CBHW071154300426
44113CB00009B/1207